Discord in Teacher-Counselor Relations

Cases from the teacher's view

GERALD KUSHEL

District Director of Guidance Services
for the Teaneck Public Schools
Teaneck, New Jersey

PRENTICE-HALL, INC., *Englewood Cliffs, New Jersey*

PRENTICE-HALL INTERNATIONAL, INC., London
PRENTICE-HALL OF AUSTRALIA, PTY. LTD., Sydney
PRENTICE-HALL OF CANADA, LTD., Toronto
PRENTICE-HALL OF INDIA (PRIVATE) LTD., New Delhi
PRENTICE-HALL OF JAPAN, INC., Tokyo

Foreword

I once asked a group of teachers at an informal gathering, "What *is* a counselor as you see him?" The answers, given in a spirit of half-jest but containing the often-bitter truth of humor, were revealing.

"If you really want to know, he's a young man bucking for vice principal."

"He's an undercover man for the administration."

"He gives all those tests and checks attendance records and calls parents. Counseling is what *he'd* like to do, I think."

"He wasn't a very good teacher, so . . ."

"He coddles the kids when they raise hell; he's Ann Landers!"

Dr. Kushel has written an intriguing casebook dealing with problems such as the ones revealed by the remarks of these teachers. Discord and misunderstanding are realities in teacher-counselor relationships. They are often serious obstacles to counselor effectiveness. This book is an attempt to present fairly and openly the perspectives of the teachers as they approach the counselor with their frustrations, hopes, needs, and aspirations.

A busy counselor may become a bit impatient or defensive when his teacher colleagues burst in on him and demand action immediately, or turn jumbled "facts" into accusations. But we must listen to the poet Gibran before we react: "You talk when you cease to be at peace with your thoughts." We counselors know this almost intuitively as we sit in the mutuality of a counseling session with a client, but we frequently do not "listen with the third ear," to use Reik's famous phrase, in dealing with our colleagues.

Instead of reacting defensively, we should look upon this expression of "peacelessness" as a welcome opportunity to re-examine our commitments and to try to see the "world of the other" just as sincerely as we do in the sessions with our clients. If the irate one had tried to find "peace with his thoughts" in a teachers' lounge, a boiler room, or over coffee, counselor effectiveness would have had no chance to improve. We must show our teacher colleagues the mutuality, the openness, and the nonjudgmental approach of which we are capable, or else suffer the loss of our most important allies. Lack of communication is, I believe, the most frequent cause of teacher-counselor conflict. It is our duty to apply what we know to be effective in a counseling session to the vital matter of dealing with teachers, parents, and administrators. We must show by our actions that we really want to know how matters are perceived by teachers, and how they view our decisions, suggestions, and manner of communication.

Dr. Kushel's book is an interesting step in this direction. He brings to the writing and selection of the cases the insight of the scholar and the experience of one who is involved daily in the world of school counseling. The cases run virtually the whole gamut of issues and everyday problems facing school counselors. Counselors and teachers will recognize the characters in the situations. They are old friends, old memories, old triumphs—or old mistakes. They are the boy in the third row, the parent on the phone, or the hard-nosed teacher at the end of the hall. They are not the cardboard characters of contrived cases. They are real.

A major strength of the book is that the characters do not fade into thin air after one episode. They appear again as tangential characters in other cases. They move in and out of the lives of others, just as do our student clients and teacher colleagues. They reappear in the counselor's office. The reader gets to know them and to feel the tone of the school setting. This is far more meaningful than glimpsing only isolated cases which focus briefly on one issue—as casebooks usually have done. Issues grow, meld with others, become clearer or more muddled. Kushel's approach recognizes this. It is a study *in context* of human beings interacting.

The issues in theory and practice which will emerge in discussions of these cases are not limited to the excellent "issue leads" provided by the author. Under the skill of a knowledgeable discussion leader, the basic philosophical issues of the value-laden, often overwhelming task of the professional counselor will be revealed. Used in this vital, practical, and scholarly manner, the book will be of great usefulness to the profession.

CARLTON E. BECK
Associate Professor of Education, University of Wisconsin-Milwaukee

Acknowledgments

To Drs. RAYMOND PATOUILLET, CHARLES MORRIS, and ESTHER LLOYD-JONES, who helped me formulate and develop this work, and to HARRIET FOLBER, who typed the original manuscript, I express my deep appreciation.

Also, I wish to thank my friend and former colleague, JANE GRAY SEACATT, for her help and encouragement when I needed it most.

Above all, I thank my wife, SELMA, for her inspiration at every turn. She made this book possible.

Contents

Discord in
Teacher-Counselor
Relations

chapter One

Toward Improving Teacher-Counselor Collaboration

"It is hardly a secret among many teachers and guidance personnel that a rift or feeling of aloofness sometimes prevails," writes a practicing school counselor to his professional journal.[1] If one looks carefully into the guidance literature, he can find well-documented evidence of discord in teacher-counselor relations.

Has the youthful guidance profession attained sufficient maturity and confidence to examine in detail and cope with the serious implications of this kind of problem? Can both parties, teachers and counselors, *be helped* to improve their relations? This casebook has been produced on the premise that these questions can be answered affirmatively.

The growth of guidance, especially since the passage of the National Defense Education Act of 1958, Title V, has been nothing less than phenomenal. However, the movement's impact on the public schools of the land has caused certain repercussions. Increasing numbers of "those guidance people" (most of whom are former teachers) have invaded terrain that has traditionally been the sole province of the classroom teacher. As would be expected, such an invasion has been met with some degree of resistance, misunderstanding, and, in some cases, utter confusion. This lack of rapport, plus a variety of other social and psychological forces, has played havoc with effective teacher-counselor collaboration. If one presumes that such collabora-

[1] Fred Weiner, Letter to the editor, *Personnel and Guidance Journal*, 41 (May, 1963), 821.

tion is directed ultimately toward *helping students*, then the converse is also true. Ineffective collaboration *detracts from helping students. It is the student who suffers!*

Surprisingly, in most guidance textbooks there is no treatment of the problems and complexities that are often found in such collaboration efforts. This casebook, the first of its kind, addresses itself directly to these problems. The reader will find virtually every type of complication encountered in actual practice. What is more, it is written through the eyes of the invaded—the teacher.

PROCEDURES

After discussion with many practicing teachers about guidance, the author selected thirty for formal interviews. All of these interviews were tape recorded, but each interviewee was guaranteed complete anonymity. Interviews were solicited in a variety of ways: through the recommendations of practicing teachers and counselors of certain of their colleagues, through the writer's direct appeals to teachers attending graduate courses at Hofstra University and Teachers College, Columbia University, and by arrangement at the registration desks during the 1965 National Education Association Convention. It was at the NEA convention that the author was able to select teachers from various sections of the country. Teachers from Pennsylvania, Georgia, Florida, California, Oregon, Nebraska, and Ohio were interviewed, giving the study broader representation. However, most of the interviews included in this book were held in New York City suburbs, particularly those on Long Island.

Although these interviews took place in diverse locations—faculty rooms of secondary schools, classrooms and student lounges at graduate colleges, a hotel lobby, the home of the author, and, in one instance, an artist's loft—most of them were held at the home of the interviewee, where he could feel at ease. They were loosely structured and ranged in time from about one-half to two and one-half hours. The teacher-respondent had been briefed as to their nature and purpose. The briefing amplified the description given in the following letter:

Dear Classroom Teacher:
  Certainly today, as much as ever, there is room for human relationships to improve. The improvement of the human relation-

ships between the classroom teacher and the guidance counselor is the focal point of this study.

It is my aim to develop specialized training materials that will be used to help guidance counselors improve their working relationship with classroom teachers. The materials will include a series of cases that will portray actual attitudes of teachers toward guidance and guidance counselors.

Although the cases will be disguised to protect the confidentiality of the classroom teacher, the cases will attempt to capture the flavor of the actual attitudes.

I believe that you are in a position to make a major contribution to this study. I would like your help. I am interested in interviewing classroom teachers who have recently been, or are presently, in contact with secondary school guidance counselors. I would very much like to interview you, at a time and place to be agreed upon. The interview will be unstructured and no prior preparation will be necessary. Although the interview will be recorded, I guarantee complete confidentiality.

If you, or one of your colleagues, would be willing to meet with me to discuss this further, please let me know after this class, or telephone me collect.

The prospective interviewee was informed that he would be asked about his attitude toward guidance and guidance counselors, based on his contacts with guidance personnel. No prior preparation was necessary. On three occasions the writer presented a sample case to a person who wanted a clearer idea of how the interview material would be used.

Only teachers who were in secondary schools that had functioning guidance programs were utilized. A conscious effort to control certain factors was made by selecting particular teachers. Certain ones were chosen in order to maintain a reasonable balance with regard to the respondent's age, sex, subjects taught, and the level of secondary education in which the teaching took place. Hence, the respondents ranged in age from 20 years to approximately 62, with an average age of about 38. Of the 25 interviews selected as a basis for case study, 9 were with women and 16 with men. The subjects being taught at the time of the interview included science, social studies, English, mathematics, foreign language, home economics, business, physical education, speech, and fine and industrial arts. Ten of the 25 teachers were employed in junior high schools.

It should be noted that the average interviewee had taught in two or three different schools during his career. Thus, the 25 teachers represented attitudes gained from many more than the 25 schools where they were affiliated at the time of the interview. A number of the teachers had had both junior high school and senior high school experience.

The author attempted to elicit a history, as well as a current picture, of the respondent's attitudes toward and perceptions of guidance and guidance counselors. He probed for evidence of either actual or latent rifts in the teacher-counselor relationship. Those rifts would often provide the basis for a case situation in which the teachers' attitude and perceptions would be unfolded.

The technique of tape recording each interview insured accuracy. After the first few moments, the persons being interviewed showed no resistance to this method. Apparently, when there was good rapport between the interviewer and interviewee and when the person was assured of the complete confidentiality of the interview, the method of recording made little difference. Each interviewee was given explicit rights to delete any statements that he felt would endanger him. Though many confidences were divulged, only one interviewee felt sufficiently threatened by the use of the tape recorder (or by the interviewer) to request a deletion. On the other hand, permission was freely given by one interviewee for the author to use the tape recording as the basis for an open discussion in a graduate guidance course. In all cases, the author exercised great care to protect the confidentiality of the interviewee and at the same time to retain the integrity and flavor of the attitudes and situations.

Formulation of Situational Cases

Of the 30 tape recorded interviews, 25 of the most suitable were selected as the basis for the situational cases found in this book. Because of the special objectives of these cases, the following restrictions were imposed upon their design: (1) Each case attempts to render an undistorted picture of a classroom teacher's attitude toward guidance and guidance counselors; (2) the identity of the teacher is disguised; and (3) the cases are constructed to gain and to hold the attention of the reader.

Each of the above restrictions posed particular problems. The effort to present as accurate a picture as possible was considerably simplified by the obvious advantages of the tape recorder. The author was able to extend his understanding of the respondents' attitudes far beyond the knowledge gained from the original interview. Through listening critically and analytically to repeated playings and through the writing of protocols of salient sections of each of the interviews, it was possible for him to "conceptualize" the attitudes and perceptions of the respondent. Though these efforts were often painful, only after such conceptualization took place was the author then in a position to attack the problem of developing the appropriate interview material into an interesting and fitting representation of the respondents' attitudes toward guidance and counselors at work. It was necessary to create fictional persons and settings that would protect the identity of the respondent while at the same time representing his confidences with integrity. Each of the interviews seemed conducive to one of the several formulas for its unfolding. Some of the attitudes and perceptions seemed best portrayed through the use of monologue; others through dialogue, flashbacks, trains of thought, or combinations of these and other literary devices. In some cases there was somewhat more focus on an incident than in others, but all aimed at revealing the dynamics of the teacher-respondent's attitudinal structure.

The cases were written in an informal style. Whenever suitable, the exact words of the teacher-respondent were used, though their use required modification in tense, form, etc., to fit the particular situation portrayed.

Several possible ways of utilizing certain of these cases were informally tried and evaluated in a guidance course at the Graduate School of Education, Hofstra University. Finally, the writer decided upon and has recommended an approach, which is fully described in Chapter 2.

The case method has been selected as an ideal one for dealing with the complexities of teacher-counselor discord. Both the discordant conditions and the attitudes of the people are embodied in a dynamic, holistic context—the case. This method enables the student to draw from a variety of disciplines and to explore the situation from a lifelike perspective rather than in a vacuum. It is also an exceptionally useful vehicle for group discussion and role-playing. These techniques have been proven superior to the lecture method, especially in the development of interpersonal skills, which are central to the alleviation of discord in teacher-counselor relations.

chapter Two

Using
The
Casebook

Each case has been arranged in the order of the degree of positive or negative feeling toward guidance and guidance counselors that the teacher-respondent seemed to hold. The intensity of the prevailing attitude was subjectively determined by the author. The cases were rated as positive, slightly negative, substantially negative, and exceptionally negative. None of them was rated as neutral. The first case is considered positive and the last one, number 25, exceptionally negative. This arrangement affords the reader an additional insight into the relative attitude of the case protagonist. Also, when it is necessary for one reason or other to economize on time, the reader can sample as few as four cases, one from each category, that will run the gamut in protagonist attitude.

Although these cases have been designed primarily for the formal and in-service education of secondary school guidance counselors, they have proved serviceable to others as well. They have application in any education course concerning guidance that is interested in genuine problems encountered in guidance practice (e.g., the training of teachers and school administrators).

Instructors of graduate courses concerning guidance in secondary education and coordination of pupil personnel services should find this casebook particularly useful. During the spring semester of 1965 at Teachers College, Columbia University, in a course entitled *Guidance in Secondary Education*, preliminary discussion of some of the first-hand material found in one of the cases, and a presentation of some of this researcher's general observations, seemed to evoke considerable interest and enthusiasm. At the State University of New York College at Oneonta the author, as Visiting Professor in Counselor Education, employed some of these cases in courses entitled: *Principles and Practices of Guidance* and *Organization* and *Administration of Guidance Services*. Improved sensitivity to teacher and counselor relations seems an appropriate aim of many courses in counselor preparation.

These cases can act as ideal supplementary material for field work and internships in guidance. When field work or internships are not available, the casebook in its entirety can be used as a basis for bridging the gap between theory and practice for the counselor trainee. Though aimed primarily at guidance majors, the cases have value in the guidance education of non-guidance majors at both undergraduate and graduate levels. On several occasions, in a guid-ance course designed for non-majors in guidance at Hofstra Univer-sity, the author, while attempting to procure teacher interviewees for the cases, presented and helped conduct discussions of certain of these cases. Again, the cases appeared to evoke great interest, as evidenced by the degree of student participation and their later comments.

In the in-service training of counselors and of teachers, the use of this book would seem to have special merit. These cases will pose no direct threat to the discussants, which might occur if the stu-dents attempted to analyze situations drawn directly from current teacher-counselor difficulties found in their immediate setting.

The cases can be employed effectively by both an individual or a group. Greatest benefits, however, will accrue to group users inas-much as the group member is aided by the checks and balances implicit to group discussion. Also, only through group usage can the valuable technique of role-playing be employed. The independent user, however, can benefit by careful reading of the cases. He might find it interesting to write out the answers to the questions in *The Guide to Case Analysis* and after a few weeks to make another analysis, giving special attention to any discrepancies that appear between his first and second efforts.

An Approach to Studying the Cases

The following plan is meant only as a suggestion and should in no way act to discourage the user's imagination in developing his own approach to the study of these cases. Any number of valid approaches exist.

This writer has chosen to adapt a guide developed by Lloyd-Jones and staff at Teachers College, Columbia University, which makes provision for an especially intensive analysis. Their guide recommends that the student first discern the persons involved in the case. The student attempts to develop empathy with each of these persons. It is explained that empathy, a state in which one mentally enters into the feeling or spirit of a person, may help the student be less disposed to make interfering judgments about the persons, such as "I liked him," or "He was selfish." With empathy, the student might be more likely to say, "I see how he looks at the situation," or "I see how he feels."

Taking a turn "inside" each of these persons, the student is asked to imagine how he *sees* and *feels* about the other people involved in the case. He is also asked to describe how he sees and feels about the problems that are central to the case. Further, the student is asked to reflect on his own ability to feel empathy with the various persons. Through these *experiences* in empathy, it is hoped that the student will better understand each of these persons. Apprehending the multifarious points of view, the student should "be better able to move toward resolution of conflict."

With empathy for the persons, the student confronts the issues in the case. He relates ideas, information and knowledge that he has gained from his own experiences, along with discussion and study of the behavioral sciences and guidance literature, in an effort to more fully clarify and weigh these issues.

Finally, the student attempts to reach certain decisions, but not decisions in the usual sense. Instead, he considers such questions as, "What could be done next? What new ideas need to be used? What new relationshps need to be established? What new information needs to be collected?"

The Guide to Case Analysis, found at the end of this chapter, is the author's adaptation of the above procedure. It offers these specific aids:

1. A series of questions leading toward empathy with the persons in each case;
2. Leads to some of the issues derived from each case;
3. A series of questions leading toward functional decision-making for each case;

4. Role-playing suggestions aimed toward the development of a more intensive *feel* for the case persons and problem(s).

Role-playing

Because these cases are particularly conducive to role-playing, and because this technique has proven especially valuable to those who have employed it, *The Guide to Case Analysis* offers specific role-playing suggestions.

Role-playing is a natural part of life, probably beginning with the child's emulation of its parents. All of us continue to role-play each day, in one way or another. Those inexperienced with this technique sometimes view it as something mysterious and threatening. The prospective user should note that role-playing, as employed here, is *not* the specialized and sophisticated procedure that has been developed for group psychotherapy by Moreno.[1] Indeed, there are many ways to role-play. Bergman and Wright recommend the following procedures:

1. A specific problem is selected for study.
2. A human relations situation that will illustrate the problem is developed.
3. Group members volunteer to play the different roles in the problem situation.
4. The scene of the problem is set.
5. The group members who volunteered to role play in the problem situation "warm up" to their roles.
6. The group members not participating in the problem situation prepare to serve as observers.
7. The participants role-play the problem situation.
8. The role-playing is ended.
9. The participants discuss their role-playing.
10. The entire group discusses the roll-playing.
11. The discussion is summarized.[2]

It is hoped that the *"Role-playing suggestions"* appended to each case will serve to encourage the reader to use this technique. These offer two different situations, each with an appropriate cast based

[1] Jacob L. Moreno, "Role," in *The Sociometry Reader*, ed. Jacob L. Moreno (New York: The Free Press of Glencoe, Inc., 1960), pp. 80-86.

[2] Richard B. Bergmann and William M. Wright, "A Guide to Role-Playing," Doctor of Education Project Report (New York: Teachers College, Columbia University, 1955), pp. 29-44.

upon the case to which they have been appended. They are in no way meant to inhibit the user from developing the role-playing which best fits his own needs and purposes.

Since the point of view of the teacher-protagonist is well established in each case, identification with him is more accessible than with others in the case. However, with a suitable "warm-up" (procedure 5, above) the prospective role-players should be able to develop clear identities for these other persons.

The prospective role-player will probably experience some anxiety from the strain of attempting to identify with another person. In order to minimize such anxiety, a good "warm-up" is worthwhile. One proven technique is to have the group at large question the prospective player. The prospect, assuming the identity of the person he is to play, is queried about such basic information as his name, his age, and his school, and then about facts of a higher order, such as his interests, his attitudes, and his feelings toward one or another person.

Another "warm-up" technique involves letting the prospective player give an extemporaneous description of himself (as the case character), working himself into the role. Still another technique is to allow the prospect sufficient solitude to "think himself into" the part.

After the "warm-up," the role-players embark into the situation, thinking, feeling, and acting like the person with whom they have identified. The acting should be spontaneous, for it is only by *spontaneously* thinking, feeling, and acting that the unique insights attainable by this method are fully realized. In the role-playing the actor experiences how he would "feel" if he were in a similar situation.

To attain the maximum values from role-playing, each group will want to tap the resources of all of its members. The procedure calls for such group processes as selecting a topic, appointing leaders, volunteering for roles, and holding discussions.

The Guide to Case Analysis

The following suggestions and questions should help the reader attain empathy with the persons in the case, clarify and weigh the issues bearing upon the case, and make certain decisions regarding the case. It is necessary to appropriate only those suggestions that suit one's particular objectives.

Empathy

WITH THE TEACHER-PROTAGONIST

1. Role-play the case utilizing one of the *Role-playing suggestions* appended to the case. (Please note that role-playing can probably be just as effective as the last step, instead of the first step.)

2. Describe the valence (positive, negative, or neutral) and the intensity of the prevailing attitude (great, moderate, or slight) that the teacher-protagonist seems to hold toward guidance and guidance counselors.

3. What pressures seem to be acting upon the teacher-protagonist to contribute to his attitude toward guidance? Counselors in general? The counselor in the case? The other persons in the case, if any? What light can sociology, anthropology, and psychology, as well as other social science disciplines, shed on these pressures?

4. How does the teacher-protagonist seem to view himself?

WITH THE COUNSELOR IN THE CASE

1. How does the counselor in the case seem to view the teacher? How does the counselor seem to view himself? How does he view each of the other persons in the case?

2. How does the problem condition in the case affect the counselor as perceived by the counselor?

WITH OTHER PERSONS

1. What other persons do you clearly discern in the case?

2. Which of these other persons, if any, rather immediately affects the teacher-protagonist's attitude toward guidance and guidance counselors?

3. How does each person (other than the teacher-protagonist) in the case view each of the other persons in the case? How does each of these persons view himself? How does each of these persons perceive the teacher-protagonist's attitudes? If discordant conditions seem to exist, how does each of the persons perceive his own connection with these conditions?

4. With which person in the case do you most readily identify?
Why?

Issues

Consider the issues involved in the case. Appended to the case are
some *Issue leads* that identify one or more of the issues that the
case touches upon. The reader should attempt to clarify and weigh
these controversial areas by bringing to bear pertinent ideas gained
from his practical experiences and discussions and from the literature
of guidance and of the behavioral sciences, such as anthropology,
sociology and psychology.

Decision-making

Take a stand on the following questions:

1. Precisely what can the guidance counselor or his department do
to correct any misperceptions about guidance and guidance counselors
that the teacher seems to hold?

2. What are some procedures that the guidance person or department portrayed in the case could have followed to have *prevented*
the negative condition that was touched upon in the case?

3. If the guidance person or department portrayed in the case were
to know all that you know about how the teacher-protagonist thinks
and feels and had thoroughly explored the relevant issues, what (if
anything) could he do to improve the collaborative relationship?
What additional information is needed?

4. Do any teachers in your school seem to hold attitudes similar
to those held by the teacher-protagonist in the case? If so, who are
these teachers? Why do you think they hold such attitudes? Exactly
what can be done to improve the situation?

She chose the latter

Robin Hayes, a first-year teacher, was having an argument with her husband regarding the worth of guidance services. Eric, with ten years teaching experience, had little regard for the guidance program in his school. His attitude was colored by a single disenchanting experience he had with a certain counselor two years earlier. One of his better students was not favorably recommended by this counselor in a college application. Eric, feeling the act unfair, had used his own influence to get her accepted. The student was admitted, but Eric felt he had been forced to do what should have been done by the guidance office.

Robin, who taught in a different school system, tried to persuade her husband to reevaluate his attitude. "All the counselors that I've come into contact with at Grandeville seem to be marvelous persons, Eric. They've been so willing to give of themselves to help me. Honestly, I've had nothing but favorable impressions."

"That's it, Robin. Impressions!" Eric said. "But wait until you need real help."

"Well, I've had the usual amount of contact with them, I'm sure, and this last experience, I think, is representative. I was impressed."

Robin explained that she had a boy in her homeroom who was extremely resentful, particularly about accepting suggestions from anyone. Several months ago, for the second time, the boy had "flown off the handle" and had attacked another boy during her homeroom period. Robin explained that when such incidents occur in her school, the teacher has the choice of referring the student to either a "rough, tough assistant principal in charge of discipline or to a guidance

13

counselor." This time she chose the latter, and a wise choice she felt it was too. Upon talking to the boy's counselor and in reviewing the record with him, she discovered that the boy had a history of emotional upset and that it had become especially aggravated during the last two years. Two years previously the boy's mother had died. His grandmother, who came to take care of him, died the next year. The counselor had met with the boy's father and related that the father didn't seem to have any feeling at all for the boy. Robin was told of the boy's recent record: smoking, truancy, extreme sensitivity, fighting . . .

The counselor asked Robin if she would like to try a session in which she, the boy, and the counselor would "talk" about the kind of behavior that was to be expected in homeroom. Robin agreed. After the session, she was delighted with the results.

She told her husband: "The counselor had the boy do most of the talking, and the boy talked himself into a very good insight into his problem in homeroom. But what has impressed me most, Eric, is that the boy's behavior has actually improved under the guidance of this man—and there was no such improvement after the first time, when I had sent him to the assistant principal. This boy needed counseling rather than punishment, and he got it. And the counselor still sees the boy."

"An interesting story," Eric commented. "I'm grateful to this counselor, whoever he is, for making your life a little easier, Robin darling, but that's an exceptional case."

"No, Eric, it isn't! At Grandeville they give our students marvelous direction regarding vocations, technical schools, and colleges. They do careful scheduling and it shows. They help with college boards. By the way, one counselor found one of the students jumped up 150 points on his college boards, so he checked into it and discovered that someone else had taken the test for him. That shows how carefully these counselors go over the records."

"Yes, go on."

"Well, Eric, most importantly, in my school they speak to the students as human beings."

"Yes, in a 10-minute interview," Eric said sarcastically.

"Maybe it's 10 or 15 minutes, but that's a lot of time when you think of all the students they are responsible for. And sometimes, for some students, there's almost unlimited time. They're interested in what the students think and feel about things. That's better than having programs and courses jammed at them, like when we were in school."

"I guess you've got something there," Eric said.

"Eric, I wish you could talk to one of our counselors. You'd change your ideas just in speaking with them and seeing their attitude."

Role-playing suggestions

[1]

CHARACTERS	SITUATION
ROBIN HAYES, *teacher-protagonist* ERIC HAYES, *teacher and Robin's husband* HAROLD ABBOTT, *guidance counselor*	Robin and Eric Hayes have invited Abbott, one of Grandeville's "model" counselors, to their home. Eric Hayes asks Abbott many questions, putting Abbott on the defensive about guidance, but Abbott convinces Eric Hayes that guidance can perform useful services.

[2]

ROBIN HAYES HAROLD ABBOTT PETE HARKINS, *student*	Harkins, the boy who was troublesome in homeroom, is being "counseled" by Abbott and Hayes. Abbott sets the pace and focus for the session. All react in character.

Issue leads

Attitudes of experienced vs. inexperienced teachers toward guidance.

Number of times a student should be seen by the guidance counselor.

Counselor's role in meting out disciplinary punishments.

The merits of student, teacher, counselor combination conferences.

Observable improvements accruing from counseling.

case 2

True guidance

Once again Timmy Evans was charged with bullying a classmate. "Look, Mr. Tishman!" Frankie Marks complained as he lifted his pants leg and exposed two black and blue welts, each the size of a half-dollar. "This is what Timmy Evans did. Please tell him to keep away from me, Mr. Tishman, please!"

Hal Tishman had been teaching industrial arts for more than a decade and had known other students like Timmy Evans. Timmy was one of those good-looking youngsters with a winning style and boyish grin who had absolutely no capacity for self-criticism.

When Timmy Evans came bounding into Tishman's third period metalworking class, Tishman confronted him with Frankie Marks' accusation. As expected, Timmy, the essence of total righteousness, avowed his innocence. Tishman said, "Timmy, I realize that it's difficult for you to accept blame. Tell me, Tim, have you ever discussed your ability to get along with your classmates with Mr. Henning? He's an awfully good man, that Mr. Henning, Tim. And he has lots of good ideas, you know!"

"Are you kidding?" Timmy replied. "I don't have any trouble with anybody. That Frankie Marks is a dirty liar, Mr. Tishman. He brought it on himself."

Hal Tishman figured it was time to end the discussion, but he hoped he had planted a seed in Tim's mind. In addition, he would tip off George Henning, the guidance counselor, that Timmy Evans was in need of his help.

Tishman genuinely felt that George Henning could help Timmy gain some needed insight. He was determined to do his best to encourage Timmy Evans to visit the counselor.

It wasn't always this way for Hal Tishman. In fact, for many years there lurked in Tishman's mind an utter disrespect for the counselor's role. As his third period class viewed a motion picture, Tishman thought, "Oh, I figured they placed kids and figured out class sizes and all that, but I had no idea of their psychiatric functions. To me, a counselor was a person that a kid went to for some superficial and often outdated information on colleges and trade schools. The counselor would give out a few pamphlets on vocations from New York Life and that's it. Frankly, my contacts were very poor. When I was in high school, my advisor never told me about the cooperative work-study programs certain colleges offer. I undoubtedly would have embarked on an entirely different career if this counselor had given me the scoop on those colleges.

"Come to think of it, my first year of teaching gave me a rotten impression of guidance. In those days I was a little too free with my hands. No doubt about it, I shouldn't have pushed kids around. That was wrong, of course. But one day, when I pushed one of the boys just a little too hard, he ran off to complain to his guidance counselor. The counselor, according to the kid's story, said, 'Mr. Tishman must be a coward to have hit eighth graders.' What I think I resented was that the counselor never came to me. All that time, until this year, I pegged guidance as a wailing wall and had no use for it.

"I would still feel that way if it weren't for a combination of events this year. First of all, George Henning came to work here as a counselor, and he has impressed me with all of the great things he's trying to accomplish with the kids. Secondly, I'm taking this course in guidance techniques, and I'm really learning something. Wow! When I first cracked that text, I thought the writer was out of his mind. It's hard to believe that even after four years of college and over ten years in the classroom, I had no notion whatsoever that guidance was interested in such ideas as self-concepts or developmental patterns. That, I think, is a shame. Somewhere, somehow, I should have been exposed. But I wasn't, and I'm certain there are many other teachers like me. And many of them will never be exposed to these concepts. Now, this is certainly not the fault of guidance. It's a two-way street. I should have extended myself years ago to find out more about guidance. But you'd think that somewhere along the line, either in my undergraduate work or on the job, I'd be informed. But that never happened!

"True guidance is like psychotherapy. The counselor makes no value judgements. All that the student says is held in complete confidence. Even if the student says he's going to burn down the school, the counselor keeps the confidence. There has to be some place in society where a kid can work out his thoughts. Other people—teachers, the administration—make the judgments; not the counselor. I can now understand for the first time why a counselor would not, could not, reprimand a student who was complaining about a teacher. The counselor's aim is to help the student gain self-insight, not to reprimand. Very few teachers, I'm sure, truly realize this. I know I didn't.

"The counselor probes the inner depths! Now, here at Monroe, we have a part-time counselor who wants to be a buddy to the students. I know he doesn't understand the true nature of guidance. He's looking toward administration. Ridiculous? Yet he said he couldn't join the Teacher's Association because he's in administration now! Boy, is he out of it! Guidance requires very special skills. Like a surgeon. I myself would be afraid of taking on the role. It demands too much."

The film ended. The lights came on. Hal Tishman looked out over the sea of faces that was his third period class. He caught the eye of Timmy Evans. Timmy gave him a knowing wink. Hal Tishman was virtually certain that George Henning would be having an introspective visitor very shortly.

Role-playing suggestions

[1]

CHARACTERS	SITUATION
HAL TISHMAN, *teacher-protagonist* FRANK SALTER, *advisor* LE ROY ALLEN, *student*	Flashback to Tishman as a high school senior meeting with Salter, his advisor. Salter rushes Tishman through an interview regarding college admissions and Tishman, afterward, finding his friend Allen in the hallway, confides his feelings about Salter.

[2]

HAL TISHMAN   At an informal occasion,
LARRY HAMPTON, *teacher*   Tishman makes several laudatory
ARNOLD POTTER, *teacher*   remarks about the value of
                                     guidance's "psychiatric" services
                                     in the school. Hampton and
                                     Potter take issue with his praise.
                                     Tishman reacts in character.

Issue leads

Distortion in student stories about teachers and their classroom idiosyncrasies.

Courses in guidance, as part of a teacher's formal preparation.

The limits of confidentiality in the counseling relationship in the secondary school setting.

The problems of communicating to the teacher the "true" role and purposes of guidance in the secondary school.

Fine arts and fine guidance

Phyllis Mills was telling Jerry Alda, one of the art teachers, about her husband's idea. "He's planning to investigate the classroom teachers' problem with guidance and guidance counselors."

Jerry looked skeptical and said, "Frankly, Phyllis, I don't think there's anything exciting there to investigate."

"Oh, I think there is," Phyllis countered. "You see, he's found evidence in guidance literature of some real resentment on the part of some teachers toward guidance. In fact, I heard you say to Herb yesterday, 'You don't work; you're a guidance counselor!' "

"Phyllis," Jerry laughed, "I was just kidding. That was a friendly rib."

"Oh, I thought I sensed the slightest resentment."

"Oh, no, Phyllis. Herb is my friend. In fact, I have a very high regard for the guidance program and counselors here at Marshall. They're doing a fine job."

"I see, but this isn't the first school in which you've worked. Did you feel the same way at Springer?"

"Well, I never thought anything about guidance when I was there. At Springer, they had a tremendous load of students to look after. They really couldn't do a job. Guidance was simply a testing factory. They gave the group I.Q. test, the Kuder, and similar tests; then the results were simply tossed into the students' files. I don't recall their having too many personal interviews. Come to think of it, they didn't work with the kids very much at all. Guidance was the place where the statistics were kept. It was a test place, not a person place.

"I didn't have any contact with guidance. Oh, some of the counselors were friends and all, but we had no professional contacts. Guidance never filtered down to my level. What does an art teacher want with an I.Q. or a Kuder Preference anyhow?"

"Gee," Phyllis commented, "you had no real contact with guidance, did you?"

"No, but here at Marshall it's a different proposition entirely. They're doing great work!"

"Really?"

"For example, now no one has told me this officially, but I think they do an excellent job matching the personality of the student with the personality of the teacher. I've noticed that in my basic art class. There are three of us teaching basic art, and we're different types, and it's too amazing to be merly coincidence that the students are placed so appropriately. Another thing. They'll transfer a student here if the teacher suggests it and it is physically possible—just for personality reasons. I think that's great! They know the art schools, and they are doing an excellent job directing students to the right school."

"Slow down, Jerry. You're killing my husband's whole idea!"

"Furthermore," Jerry went on, "just this morning Stu Green demonstrated the worth of guidance to me again."

"In what way?"

"That little character, Sherwin Pine, was helping me backstage yesterday after school. I was working on a construction problem—trying to erect a platform near a false window. He stood there, egging me. 'It'll never work, Mr. Alda,' he said. Then, when I had turned away for the moment, he jumped up on it. Naturally, it fell. What a thud; what a mess! In front of eight other kids he gibed, 'I told you, Mr. Alda, it wouldn't work.' I told him, 'Sherwin, if you're not going to work, please leave.' 'I told you it wouldn't work,' he said again. 'I know more than you, Mr. Alda.' Then I blew up. I said to Pete Morenda, who was directing, 'Throw him off the stage. Get him out of my sight!' The kid just stood there—completely insubordinate. Finally Morenda got rid of him for me.

"This morning at 7:45 I left a note with Stu Green telling about the incident and that I didn't want Sherwin Pine in my class today. You know what? Stu saw Sherwin already, had a nice chat with him, and Sherwin wasn't in during sixth period. Now, that's active guidance."

"Wasn't this more of a discipline case for the administration?" asked Phyllis.

"No, I don't think so. You see, this is a learning problem that Sherwin is having. Besides, I've been involved with Stu regarding Sherwin for months."

"Oh."

"So, Phyllis, guidance is all right by me."

"But wait, Jerry, I've heard you complain that you're not getting the kind of kids in your classes you think art can help."

"That's true. However, I'm not sure it's guidance at fault. I think it's more a part of our whole society. For example, Phyllis, you once told me that your husband paints as a *hobby*. Now the way you said that seemed to imply that to paint for a *career* wasn't really respectable. Art is almost a dirty word. Art doesn't really count.

"I wish the guidance people would channel some of those burly football types into art courses. I see them taking shop courses but rarely the fine arts. Yet, when they do take art, we can often get them to catch fire.

"And the high I.Q.'s. How about those youngsters? Guidance encourages those kids to stick to the heavy academics. If they want to take something extra, guidance says, 'Take an enriched chemistry course.' I think it was the 1957 report from M.I.T. that recommended that all engineering applicants have a course in the creative arts in their background. I never hear anyone in guidance quoting that report. Guidance says, 'Oh, the colleges want all the academics.' Still, when I talk to the college teachers, they say they want kids with some creative background. I don't think the college admissions people and the college professors are in agreement.

"Anyway, guidance doesn't promote art. They may not deliberately sabotage the art program, but I cannot say they actively promote it. I wish they would."

"Say," Phyllis smiled, "you don't have a completely benign attitude after all."

Role-playing suggestions

[1]

CHARACTERS

JERRY ALDA, *teacher-protagonist*
CARLTON LACE, *artist-teacher*

SITUATION

At Lace's art studio, while Lace is painting, Alda comments upon the "low regard for fine arts held by the common man." Lace thinks "the schools are greatly to blame." Alda, in character, describes a plan for the guidance department in their school to upgrade the fine arts program.

[2]

JERRY ALDA
PHYLLIS MILLS, *teacher*
JACK MILLS, *Phyllis' husband*

Alda is being interviewed by Jack Mills, for Mills' doctoral study (described in the case). Alda, reacting in character, speaks freely.

Issue leads

The value of standardized testing to an art teacher.

Matching students with certain teachers.

The guidance counselor's role in discipline.

The extent that a guidance counselor should "promote" a particular course.

Art for Jonathan Longly

Dad passed away eight years ago. I'm all alone now, but I'm not really lonely. Almost every night I have visitors. Sometimes people wonder how an old woman like me manages in such a big house, but I honestly don't mind it! Dad's presence is still here, and of course there's my work. It's truly a great responsibility. I love the children. They keep me young! I've been teaching now for over 37 years, and I've taught everything. You name it!

If my father hadn't been a professional artist, I don't think that I would ever have had any interest in Jonathan Longly. He was on the ornery side, and nothing that I or any other teacher did for him seemed to make him respond. But one day I brought some of my dad's work into my biology class, and you should have seen Jonathan light up when he discovered that I was interested in art. In biology, the students had to do their drawings right from the specimens. I wouldn't let a student copy a picture out of a book. If you're going to learn about crayfish, put it down, no matter how crude the drawings. Jonathan really had talent, and his drawings were beautiful.

Unfortunately, he came from the Harrison Park section—over the tracks. Oh, Jonathan was no student! Frankly, he was a troublemaker in most classes, but he had a job after school, and he worked hard.

As soon as he graduated from high school, he planned to go out and get just any job. We had some long talks, and I was able to convince him to consider going to an art school, at least part time, after he graduated.

I went down to the guidance department to get some information on art schools for him. After speaking to his so-called counselor, Nora Trout, down there, I felt as if I had hit my head against a stone wall. "This is ridiculous," Nora said. He was a troublemaker; he was stupid; he was everything! "Be glad when he's out! Let's get rid of him," she said. "This boy is better off just getting a job in a garage."

She had an awful lot of trouble with students like Jonathan. Nora was a former English teacher, and if a youngster didn't speak perfectly, and if he looked as if he came from the wrong side of the tracks, all interest was lost. I love people, including Nora, and I don't think her actions were directed personally at me at all. She just thought I was being silly and that Jonathan was "taking me for a ride," as she expressed it. If he had come down looking well dressed and well polished and had spoken beautifully, we wouldn't have had this little fracas.

In spite of Nora, I went ahead. I pushed and pushed and pushed. At that time my Father was living, and Dad *knew* people. We, Dad and I, got that boy into an art school. Jonathan Longly worked and took night courses. What he's doing now, I don't know. I haven't heard from him lately, but he was doing *all right,* last I heard!

Role-playing suggestions

[1]

CHARACTERS	SITUATION
VIRGINIA GRAYSON, *teacher-protagonist* DAD GRAYSON, *Virginia's father* JONATHAN LONGLY, *student*	The Graysons have invited Longly to their home, hoping to inspire him into pursuing an art education after graduation. Longly, reluctant at first, eventually expresses some interest.

[2]

VIRGINIA GRAYSON
NORA TROUT, *guidance counselor*

In the guidance office Trout explains to Grayson that Longly isn't worth all the time and effort that Grayson is expending. Trout refers to Longly's poor record and untidy appearance. Grayson, in character, takes exception.

Issue leads

The teacher's contribution in the guidance of students to post-high school education.

A teacher's and a counselor's contrasting perception of the same student.

A *total job*

The curls of smoke filled the kitchen and seemed to hover around the bright, fluorescent-lit ceiling. The pennies and nickels clinked irregularly and became interwoven with the shuffling of cards, the brisk and husky talk of the players, and the occasional "pfft" of the escaping gas from the freshly-opened beer cans. This was the semi-monthly poker game.

Calvin Dorn, the baby-food salesmanager, complained, "You teachers have it too good."

Abe Wolfson, a teacher, jokingly poked the player seated to his left and winked at him. "Check him. If you really want a racket, Cal, you should become a guidance counselor."

The players were ready for a brief recess, and all the cards were tossed into the center of the kitchen table. "Yeah," Carl Highland chipped in, "there's a real racket for you." Several others, who were apparently in the school business, nodded agreement.

"What do you mean, a racket?" Cal Dorn asked, now in a serious manner.

"Well, Cal, actually there are two types in guidance; there are the guidance *persons* and there are the guidance *counselors*. These fellows are talking about guidance *persons*," explained Chester Berlin, a health and physical education teacher at the local Cromwell High School. Dorn, the salesman, and Highland, librarian at Cromwell High, were eager to pursue Chet's explanation. The three of them stepped from the noise of the kitchen to the relative quiet of the living room.

28

"What do you mean, there are two types in guidance: persons and counselors?" asked Dorn, with a puzzled look.

"Is that something you got out of those guidance books you've been borrowing from our professional library? Say, I hope you're not getting any foolish ideas about going into guidance, are you, Chet?" added Highland.

"Look, boys, let's get things straight. One—I'm not getting any ideas about going into guidance, and two—no, these two types I've mentioned haven't come from any books."

"Well, come on, then, explain what the difference is between guidance counselors and guidance persons."

"Guidance *persons* are the objective, cold types that the others are talking about. They do the paper work; they administer mass tests. They're gobbed up in schedules. You get objective things from them: test scores, student locations, board scores, and so on. Carl, we're all trained to be objective, and with a little effort, any of us can do the same. But, Carl, I've been in three different schools in my ten years in this business and have been exposed to quite a few people in guidance. To my mind, most of them were guidance *persons*. There were only two guidance *counselors* among them: one in my first school, and the other here in Cromwell."

"What were they like, these counselors?"

"Cal, these two did things that couldn't be achieved in any classroom. Take Wayne Slocum, the first one: he was a one-man department. When I read that book I borrowed last week by this Rogers, I was reminded of Wayne Slocum. Slocum personified Roger's ideas. There's not enough of that going on. Slocum would be running his head off down the halls; he wasn't just a bookkeeper. He'd let the piles of paper build up. If a kid came to him, knocked on his door, and said he wanted to talk, Wayne Slocum would make time for him. Oh, the papers piled up. He was untidy; but the kids were attracted to him. He brought the kids in and gave them something. All the things you read in books, he put into practice. He didn't feel threatened. You could talk with him about anything."

"Non-directive?" Carl asked.

"Well, he didn't try to tell them what to do! I grew in my own handling of kids by working with him, by watching him, seeing him operate, hearing the things he said and how he said them. I was 21 years old then; I grew from him—just like I'm going to grow from the person I'm working with now."

"You're referring to Ann Halsey in our school, aren't you?"

"Yes. I never would have known what a great counselor she is if it weren't for the situation with that senior, Kenny Martin. Kenny's dad came to me and bluntly told me that he couldn't handle his own kid. Could I help him?"

"Did you?"

"I thought I could, but I wasn't getting anywhere. That's when I went to Ann Halsey. She's great. She did a *total* job."

"What do you mean, a *total* job?"

"Well, she spent a lot of time talking to Kenny's teachers, not only from the high school but from the elementary school as well. She read between the lines in the reports. Then she told me, 'Chester, you can do something; he looks up to you.' From her I've been able to get kinds of ways and kinds of approaches."

"Specify."

"Well, what to say and how to say it to the kid."

"For instance? Chet, you haven't really said anything specific."

"For instance, I would not have known that Kenny's a distrustful soul; that he can't get close to anyone. Ann indicated to me that I could get him to trust me and be free with me and talk with me— just visit—that I could help. I didn't know this about Kenny. Also, she indicated that Kenny's father really was pressing him. I didn't realize that. I thought his dad was a pretty good Joe. She indicated that something.was going on in the family. As I said, she gave me the impression that she was doing a total job. Now we're working on this boy together, trying not to let him know that we're a team."

"Honestly, Chet, don't you think that you, as a coach and phys ed man, do more guidance than those guidance folk?"

"Boys, that's the better part of coaching. We guide. We get a chance to see the kids at their heights, when they've won a game, and at their low points when they've lost and have made mistakes. Not many teachers or counselors have that chance. What gripes me most is seeing people who I know were not top-notch teachers move right up the ladder through guidance. Actually, when I think of it, I haven't heard many good things being said about guidance in my years as a teacher: at meetings, conferences, classes at C.U. 'Oh, those guidance people!' There's not much respect for them. But honestly, Carl, these two counselors, Halsey and Slocum, were really good ones. They were warm persons. By the way, did you know that Ann Halsey is an ex-phys ed teacher?"

"You're just partial," said Cal with a smile as he stepped into the kitchen and began to gather the cards together on the table. "Come on, gang," he hollered. "How about seven card stud?"

Role-playing suggestions

[1]

CHARACTERS | SITUATION

CHESTER BERLIN, *teacher-protagonist*
CARL HIGHLAND, *school librarian*

Several days after the case situation, Berlin confides to Highland that he is seriously considering "going into guidance." Highland tries to discourage Berlin. Berlin reacts in character.

[2]

CHESTER BERLIN
WAYNE SLOCUM, *guidance counselor*
ANN HALSEY, *guidance counselor*
CALVIN DORN, *salesman*

At an informal gathering at Berlin's home, Dorn describes the high regard that Berlin said he held for both Slocum and Halsey. Slocum and Halsey, in turn, react in character, describing certain of their thoughts about what they are trying to accomplish as guidance counselors.

Issue leads

The adequacy of a classroom teacher's training for properly interpreting standardized test results.

The adequacy of a guidance counselor's training for properly interpreting standardized test results.

The advisability of the guidance counselor "getting around the building."

The strength of a guidance counselor's general influence on classroom teachers.

Teacher-counselor collaboration, without the student being so informed.

A description of the details involved in doing a "total job" in the guidance of a particular student.

Student personality and behavior, as observed outside rather than inside the classroom.

A good cuff on the ear

How can a counselor help anyone? Even the good ones are steeped in a lot of book work—tiny essentials—and they don't have enough time to be really interested in their counselees. They have scheduling a certain time during the year. They have to see the sophomores at one time and the juniors another time, and they are busy answering questions about programs and college boards and what college Johnnie should go to and all that.

The real problem kids, somehow, are dropped by the wayside. I learn most about my problem kids from the other teachers when we have group meetings after school, not from the counselors. It's very helpful to talk with the other teachers. Much useful information has come to light. But the few times that I've sat down with just a counselor to discuss my class lists, his information has been very sketchy. Meeting with the other teachers is the best help. Of course, this can be overdone too, but it never has been—here, at least.

The students who are underachievers and are real psychological problems could certainly stand some talking to on a friendly basis. They're being neglected, sometimes because the counselors are so busy with the other essentials, but more often, I think, because the wrong kinds of guys are in guidance. You know, I'm not sure if many of the people that I've met in guidance are really cut out for it.

I've had some experiences with guidance that were rather frustrating. Sometimes, like all teachers, I have a student I can't seem to reach. I don't have the training or the knowledge or the time to dig into his problem. Unfortunately, guidance isn't usually able to help me either. They're too busy with other things, or they're not really interested. Most often I have to seek after them. This year I've had a couple of nasty experiences that prove my point.

You see, we get referral slips, you know; requests for information. I got one this year: "How long have you known John Z? What can you tell me about him?" It wasn't even signed by the counselor. Not recognizing the handwriting, I stopped by the guidance office and simply asked, "Who sent this, please, and what kind of information is wanted?" Finally I was put in touch with the guidance counselor who wrote it. He said to me, "I don't care what you write. A social worker is coming to see me. Put down anything you feel like putting down." I said, "What do you mean? Social adjustment? Grades? What would you like me to stress? Are you planning to move the student to a different grouping or what?" He answered, "Miss Whitman, I don't know. I know nothing about it."

This student has been in our district for at least three years. There obviously was a record. If the counselor was interested, he would have known or at least would have been able to find out something about the situation. It eventually turned out that the student was a foster child, and the social worker was just checking on his social adjustment, but I had to take the initiative and go back to the counselor and ask what happened, after about three or four days had gone by. There's very little initiative taken by guidance.

Of course, not all of the counselors are that way. There are some exceptions, but these exceptions seem to be in the minority. By and large the counselors aren't too helpful, although we do have one who really tries to help. He'd make a very good assistant principal, but he makes a very poor guidance counselor. Poor soul! He's interested, but I think in the wrong way.

Once, when I had a student who was troublesome—the kind that stands up in class, runs to the front of the room every five minutes, sharpens his pencil, trots around—I said to myself, "I'm sure there's something wrong with this boy." I mentioned him to this particular counselor one day in the faculty room. The counselor was having his usual second coffee break. I told him that the boy seemed to be having real problems. I told him how one day the boy had said, "Oh, don't flunk me, Miss Whitman, my mother will kill my pet!" I had said, "Kill your pet? What are you talking about?" And the boy had said, "She'll throw my dog out the window!" Well, this was a very serious problem for the boy. I said to the counselor, "You know, this boy *is* a real problem and also *has* real problems. Can't something be done?" I was hoping that the counselor would take the first step and then the next step would be the school psychologist, who would work with him. I was going through channels. Well, the next day I went into the office to see this so-called counselor. With a big smile on his face, he said to me, "Miss Whitman, I took care of your problem for you!" How wonderful, I thought, but only momentarily. He went on and said, "I had the boy down here. I swatted him and I said, 'Why are you giving Miss Whitman trouble?'"

So, I found that when you have a problem child, bringing it to the attention of this particular counselor wasn't going to help. I guess there will always be people like him who have been years and years in teaching and now want a change of pace, so they find themselves a guidance job without having any flair or understanding of it whatever. For them, all guidance means is programming and a good cuff on the ear!

Role-playing suggestions

[1]

CHARACTERS	SITUATION
SALLY WHITMAN, *teacher-protagonist* JOHN BROOKS, *guidance counselor* SETH CARLINS, *math teacher* THERESA CODY, *school nurse* CAROL SCHIELDS, *English teacher*	Acting upon Whitman's request, Brooks calls a meeting regarding a particular student. Brooks is not familiar with the student or his record, while the others—Carlins, Cody, and Schields—have many valuable suggestions for Whitman, based on their observations and contacts with the student; Whitman reacts.

[2]

SALLY WHITMAN
CHARLIE GUNTHER, *guidance counselor*
MRS. MANUS, *guidance secretary*

Whitman visits the guidance office in response to the request for information about a certain student (see case). Whitman and Gunther, the counselor who sent the unsigned note, re-enact the encounter as described in the case.

Issue leads

The soundness of regularly scheduling guidance sessions between teachers and counselors.

The guidance information that one teacher can provide for another.

The need for faculty to be more friendly to students.

The difficulties faced by the teacher who would like to explore intensively the background of a problem student.

The effects of poorly written communications.

My extra help

Blanche's first two years of teaching were in the very high school from which she had graduated. Her former teachers, turned colleagues, provided her, as a math teacher, with a friendly and protective entree into the business of teaching. Blanche believed also that guidance and guidance counselors made a major contribution to the school and to the students. Perhaps a special reason for her attitude was the "sensible and discreet" help guidance had provided for her sister and parents some years before, when her sister was "in trouble with a boy and had to leave school." This experience set a tone for a very positive view of guidance and guidance counselors. Positive, that is, until she took that teaching job "out East."

Blanche's first year at Terris Junior High, near Trenton, was marred by a particular guidance person. This was Blanche's story:

"Mrs. Ralston had been at Terris Junior High for some time, and she was rather respected in the town. She was in her forties—quite a bit older than I was—with many more years in education than I.

"One of her favorite counselees was in my algebra class. His name was Jordan Daniels, and he wasn't doing very well. I became a little bit concerned about his performance, so I took it upon myself to discuss Jordan's difficulties with Mrs. Ralston. She was concerned too and offered to do anything she could do to help. We decided that I should send Jordan's quiz papers home and should keep her continuously informed as to Jordan's progress. Jordan came in after school regularly, for extra help. Mrs. Ralston, Jordan, and I even had a special conference together to try to help Jordan.

"In spite of all the help, Jordan didn't seem to be making much progress. He was, I think, a little bit immature in class. He and some of his friends caused some disruptions. Jordan seemed to feel that I was unfair in that I called his attention to things he should have been doing a bit more often than I did for some of his friends. That's what he expressed to Mrs. Ralston.

"We worked as well as we could, but we didn't seem to be making much progress. Suddenly I received a notice that Jordan was transferring. He came in with a change of schedule form. I said, "Jordan, I'm sorry to see that you are going. Why is this?" He said, "Oh, it's because of my science class. There's something that I have to change in science."

"Well, I knew that he was also having difficulty in science. As the year progressed, however, I got the idea that while he told me that it was because of science class, there were some math class reasons also. I had the feeling that his mother and Mrs. Ralston decided that they would prefer him to have some other teachers. Both the science teacher and I were new at Terris Junior High School. His second teachers were long time acquaintances of Mrs. Ralston!

"At the end of the year, I was interested in seeing how Jordan had done. He passed the course, but he actually didn't do any better with the second teacher than he had been doing with me. In fact, one marking period Jordan got a lower grade in his second math class than he had in mine. That is some proof that it wasn't simply a personality clash between Jordan and me. Naturally, I felt a bit unhappy about the matter. But even if Mrs. Ralston had orginated this change, the incident by itself wouldn't have been too bad. I could let it pass.

"But then, during the same year, I had a conflict with another student's mother. His mother was angry because her son was failing. In his particular class he was one of the very few who were failing. It was a pretty alert group. After several discussions regarding her son's problems, the mother demanded that she and I discuss our differences with the principal. This was fine, as far as I was concerned. When we met with the principal, the mother mentioned that her son had come to me for extra help a couple of times, as I had suggested. She said that he wasn't getting anything from my suggestions. Then she said, 'By the way, Mrs. Ralston mentioned that the same situation had occurred with one of her other counselees. This other student didn't seem to get anywhere either. . . .'

"Well, this made me a little bit upset. Honestly, I have other students who have taken advantage of my help sessions and, because of great diligence on their part, have raised their averages as much as twenty-five points. I knew that my help was of some value if the children tried and were consistent in utilizing the help I offered them. To think that this counselor had told this parent that I was having a problem with my help sessions! I didn't think that this was a very professional thing to have done, without my knowledge. Mrs. Ralston hadn't heard my side of the story about this boy's progress. How could she have done such a thing? Okay. Well, that was the second situation, and I wasn't too happy about it.

"The next problem was with a very capable girl. She should have been doing well in algebra. Somehow, she was having a struggle. Halfway through the quarter, I sent out an interim report and indicated several things that I thought might help her to improve. One suggestion was that she come in for extra help. I felt that since she had been absent quite often and had missed several key sessions, she might get the material she had missed. For the most part, she was a responsible girl. She too was called in by Mrs. Ralston, and the two of them talked about algebra. Afterwards, this student came up to me and said, 'I've talked to my counselor about the interim report you sent out. She suggested that I should talk with you to see what I can do to improve.' I said to her, 'Carolyn, you haven't been in for extra help. I would suggest that you do come for it, because you've been absent so often.' She said, 'Well, my counselor said than another student was in for extra help and it didn't do him much good. She doesn't think that extra help is for me either, especially since I have so many important after-school activities.'

"So—that just made me very upset. After all, this youngster had been absent! Mrs. Ralston just wasn't justified. The other two children weren't like this girl. They needed extra attention *besides* what was given in class. But this girl had been absent. It wasn't the same.

"I've been a little bit shy to say anything about it. I've just resolved that when I go back to Terris Junior High School next year, if I have any of Mrs. Ralston's counselees and if they're doing poorly, I will keep her very well informed. And if she repeats her actions next year, I shall certainly discuss my problem with the principal. I'm not interested in bringing this up as gossip. Mrs. Ralston has an excellent reputation, and there's no question but that the students respect and enjoy her very much. But she really hurt me."

Role-playing suggestions

[1]

CHARACTERS	SITUATION
BLANCHE WATSON, *teacher-protagonist* HELEN RALSTON, *guidance counselor* LARRY HEITE, *principal*	After the case situation occurs once again, Ralston's actions have "hurt" Watson. After hearing of the incident, Heite calls the two women to his office to "iron out" their differences.

[2]

BLANCHE WATSON ENID YALES, *teacher* MARGE NOBLE, *teacher*	Watson, Yales, and Noble are discussing school. Watson describes her "problems" with guidance. Noble suggests she speak directly with Ralston. Watson breaks down.

Issue leads

The extent that a counselor should discuss a teacher's alleged or real shortcomings with a parent.

Times when a student's class should be changed, without informing the teacher.

Counselors as mediators of teacher-parent-student relationships.

A teacher is waiting

"Damned if I'm going to kill the rest of my lunch period waiting for Ashwin to give me a few minutes! I'll live without the information! The hell with it!" thought Goodwin Halsey, a teacher, as he informed counselor John Ashwin's secretary that he "just *had* to go to lunch or starve!" This simple event lapsed into the limbo of Halsey's unconscious for the next several years until Lionel Tepper rescued it.

Halsey had attended a summer session at Tulane with Lionel Tepper and had begun to appreciate Lionel, "even if the kids don't." Halsey thought, "Lionel wasn't cut out to be a classroom teacher. He was always concerned that he wasn't affecting his students personally. He wanted to be important and liked by his students. He wanted, desperately, to have more effect on people in general. But Lionel couldn't even control his classes. Poor fellow, he couldn't ever be a disciplinarian. Just a helpful old soul! And because of school politics and the hapless power structure, he was always ending up on the short end of the stick." Halsey really felt pity for Lionel as they commuted back and forth that summer and talked about school. "There was poor old Lionel, suffering away in the classroom and perhaps, though probably not, he might have been a very good teacher years before. Now a really good teacher can affect youngsters plenty; he doesn't necessarily have to make everything such a personal battle! Not everything in class has to be a personal struggle between the student and the teacher. The good teacher doesn't dwell on pure personality. And he doesn't always applaud or bawl out a youngster

41

on a personal basis. 'John, you disappoint *me!*' or 'Do it for *me*, John.' The good teacher puts his judgment on a higher plane than the personal. And he can win confidence out of fear or love and have a great, winning effect on the youngster." These were Halsey's ideas about good teaching. And these were qualities quite the opposite of Lionel Tepper's.

So, a couple of years later, when the guidance movement hit the South and Lionel Tepper was picked as one of the persons to be added to the guidance department, Halsey was delighted and relieved for his friend. "Thank heaven, he'll be away from all those discipline problems that he couldn't handle," Halsey figured. "Lionel is a good man. He has a definite feeling for these kids and sincerely wants to help. His new job isn't going to be at all like teaching. He's got to be around to listen, to not listen, to work with, to not work with, to encourage, to deter, to help, to sometimes hinder, and to respect the youngster's wishes. Man, it's really hard to pinpoint his new job. I don't know. The textbooks are full of what guidance is. Lionel has got to be someone that the student can go to and get individualized information on any subject that has relevance to school or even out-side of school. And this is a face-to-face contact. This is where Lionel will excel. He has the ability to gain understanding, to listen, to keep his mouth shut and to let things soak in. I think the students will realize that Lionel is a true helper and not just a pseudo-helper."

Guidance started out on a very temporary basis at Wingate High, and the administration, as well as people like Lionel Tepper, didn't entirely realize what guidance was to be. Some very qualified people did get into guidance work, but quite accidentally. Such was Lionel's case.

Time passed, and one day it was necessary for Goodwin Halsey to consult Lionel about a student. When he stopped by the guidance office, the secretary said, "Mr. Tepper is in conference, Mr. Halsey, but I'll buzz him. Mr. Tepper has instructed me to notify him im-mediately when any teacher is waiting to see him."

And then it hit Halsey—the time he had given up waiting for John Ashwin.

Role-playing suggestions

[1]

CHARACTERS

GOODWIN HALSEY, *teacher-protagonist*
LIONEL TEPPER, *guidance counselor*
JOHN FENTON, *Halsey's friend*

SITUATION

Halsey, Tepper, and Fenton, upon an informal occasion, discuss guidance. Tepper describes how much he enjoys being a guidance counselor. Halsey explains to Fenton that Tepper "couldn't teach very well."

[2]

GOODWIN HALSEY
ASHWIN JONES, *guidance counselor*

In Jones' office Jones asks Halsey why he rarely makes referrals. Halsey reacts openly but in character.

Issue leads

The lengths to which a counselor should go to make himself available to teachers.

The contrast between the optimal personal qualities required by teachers and those required by counselors.

Guidance's role in discipline.

The possibility that weak teachers are often "made" guidance counselors.

case 9

Watered geometry

It was "Professional Day" at Thorton High. One full day in the middle of each academic year was set aside for the faculty to discuss philosophical issues, hear a guest speaker, and then hold meetings to discuss departmental curriculum problems.

Ned Farrell, of the guidance department, stepped into the room where the math department was meeting. The discussion was centered on the 10th-grade geometry course. Joe McElroy, head of the math department, had evidenced concern that there were so many mid-year failures. It was at this point that Farrell made the following suggestion: "Perhaps for next year you folks might consider offering two courses in geometry: one for the students with some math ability and the other one for the weaker students—the type of student that is failing now."

"Yes," one of the teachers replied, "but how would the colleges look at the weaker course?"

The counselor suggested that the school might offer the two courses, using a code to help Thorton differentiate between them, but have an identical title for both courses on transcripts to colleges. It was then time for the session to break for lunch. "Let's pick this discussion up right here after lunch," said McElroy.

Over lunch the math teachers continued the discussion informally. Ned Farrell was dining elsewhere.

"Farrell's notion about another kind of geometry course for the poorer math students sounds all right, but it just isn't practical," Joe McElroy said. "Ned Farrell's problem is—and I can say this, because I've known him for 29 years—he hasn't kept up with the math and doesn't understand it. He used to teach math 25 years ago, but he doesn't understand, really understand, the terrific changes that have taken place in math programs all over the country."

"I kind of doubt that he doesn't understand the present math programs," one of the teachers conjectured. "I just think he doesn't have the math interests at heart."

"Yes, you've got something there," Joe went on. "Farrell suggested that we water down the geometry course because of the high failure rate. His solution seems to be, 'If you make the courses easier, you won't have so many failures. Then we won't have so many parents on our backs and everybody will be happy!' Of course we can't water the math course! These kids simply don't belong in geometry X. If the guides want to let them go in there, it's perfectly all right, but they'll either pass or fail on their own merits."

Jane Minardi, one of the newer math teachers, asked, "Exactly what do these guides do?"

Joe responded, "Well, Jane, I'm not too sure, but I do know that the guides are terribly overworked, for one thing. I don't think we have enough of them. Lots of clerical work has been pushed their way. We would be hard-pressed to guide just the kids we have in our classes, and each guide has about three times that number. Jane, you've probably noticed that our math department keeps close contact with the guidance department here at Thorton. I, personally, find they come to me more often than I go to them, which I feel is good. Whenever they have a problem on placement in mathematics, for instance, they will come to me. I rely on them for a great deal of information about the student involved, so we thrash out the problem together. You know, whatever is best for the child. I enjoy working with most of these people. All in all, they're a pretty good group. I sort of guide the guides. Ha, ha!"

"Sounds good."

"It wasn't always this way. There was a time when the guides would place the children, and then they'd get in trouble and come hollering for help. It finally got to the point where the guides talked to me first."

"Why do you always call them guides, Joe, when they're really called counselors?" asked one of the teachers.

"I guess I'm dating myself. Guides are what counselors used to be called. For some reason or other, somebody thought it was better to call them counselors instead of guides. But all my life I've referred to them as guides. That's what they do, don't they? Guide people? Or at least they attempt to! Maybe a counselor isn't quite the same, is it?"

"No, Joe, I don't think that 'counselor' means the same thing. 'Counselor' sounds deeper."

"I'm not sure if our guides know enough about areas other than guiding kids to colleges. After all, their backgrounds have been almost purely academic. Anything they've learned about the non-college-bound student probably came out of a textbook or a lecture or something like that. Having been through the college experience themselves—having applied and gained admission to college and associating mostly with college people—they have a better knowledge of procedures and colleges.

"Not that we don't need *counselors* rather than guides. The point is, do we really have those specialists, or do we just have people? Did we hire unqualified people because someone like Conant said we need more counselors, but there were only *people* available, not counselors? It seems to me a counselor should be trained as a priest or minister would be trained. Clergymen are made to spend time in the old folks' home and similar places, because when they graduate, they have to know what the story is. I don't think we train our guides that way. We just have them take courses. They're not really equipped.

"A friend of mine from South Lane had a boy in his social studies class who couldn't read. So he sent the kid to guidance or the educational clinic—whatever they called it. They sat and tested this guy for three weeks, and my friend got the report back. The report said, 'The kid can't read!' He *knew* this to start with, so what was accomplished? You see, there is quite a bit of pretense here.

"As you know, Jane, every teacher is supposed to be a guide. And every teacher probably does a certain amount of guiding along the lines in which he is qualified. Guidance people should stick to what they are qualified in too. Red Claster, the distributive education teacher, has the program where the students go out and work for half a day. Now, he gives them guidance. He tells them how to act in the interview and on the job. Come to think of it, he probably gives more 'real' guidance to the kids that need it most than does the whole guidance department, and he guides in an area where he is qualified.

"But college is the thing in this community, and helping the kids get into college seems to be the major enterprise of guidance. We've got math courses for the non-college student, but in this community we have a hard time convincing the kids and their parents that the course is for them. Today, it seems, everyone wants to go to college."

The afternoon session of the math meeting brought a return to the problems raised by Ned Farrell: Should there be two courses of geometry offered to meet the needs of the capable and the weaker students? If so, how should they be labeled on the transcripts to college? The discussion brought out a feeling that eventually all students, even the good ones, would end up in the weaker course if the titles were the same because of the pressure for grades by the colleges. Farrell, in defense of his earlier proposal, said, "The trouble is that certain children just do not have math ability, and yet they are good in many other fields. These children are being denied the right to go to college because they can't pass the math sequence."

Joe McElroy somewhat heatedly responded, "First of all, Ned, this is not *our* problem. It's the colleges' problem. They're the ones that make the rules. Math hasn't kept kids out of college—just certain prestige colleges. It's not that these students couldn't get into *a* college, but that they couldn't get into *the* college. I know that this is a tough problem for you fellows. But your suggestion about watering the math course down will destroy the reputation that we've built up over 35 years. If you water the courses down, you can get away with it for just so long, and before you know it—pfft—nobody will take the kids anymore."

Role-playing suggestions

[1]

CHARACTERS	SITUATION
JOE MC ELROY, *teacher-protagonist* NED FARRELL, *head of guidance* BERT JUDSON, *math teacher*	After the meeting, Farrell continues to try to convince McElroy to offer "another kind" of geometry for the weaker students. McElroy weakens. Judson approves of Farrell's suggestion.

[2]

JOE MC ELROY   McElroy explains to Lokken
RAY LOKKEN, *principal*   that "guidance wants to weaken
                                           my course." Lokken tries to
                                           explain the guidance position.

Issue leads
The degree of influence that colleges have
on secondary school curricula.

The use of deceptive course titles.

The extent to which a counselor needs to comprehend the
"modern math" program.

The appropriateness of the title "guide" rather than "guidance counselor."

Is every teacher a guidance counselor?

The proctors

There will be a special meeting of all teachers who are to proctor the Iowa Achievement Tests, Wednesday morning at 8:15 in the cafeteria—Helen Devor, Head of Guidance

Thirty teachers were seated in the cafeteria, but quite a few were still missing. It was already 8:17, so Helen Devor thought she had better begin. The teachers had to be in their homerooms at 8:40.

Mrs. Devor, a personable woman in her mid-forties, of slight build, spoke out in a pleasant voice. "Faculty, can I have your attention, please? This morning we are going to cover the procedures for administering the Iowa Achievement Tests. What we are to discuss here is very important, so please give me your kind attention."

The teachers grew quiet. Mrs. Devor spent the next twenty minutes conscientiously covering the procedures for administering the Iowa tests which would be given later that day. The results would be important to students, parents, counselors, and teachers alike.

After school, young and shapely Elaine Roper, the dramatics and speech teacher, waved to her husband as his car pulled to the curb outside. Ted worked nearby and almost always drove Elaine home from school. This helped these newlyweds' budget. Besides, they enjoyed traveling together.

"Hi, darling!" Ted said as Elaine hopped into the car. Once on the road, he asked, "Well, how was the big meeting this morning?" He was curious, because he had had to get Elaine up half an hour earlier that morning so she could be on time for the meeting.

"It was, I am sorry to say, a complete waste of time!" she replied. "Quite a few of the other faculty members felt the same way. It was an insult."

"Why were you so insulted?"

"Well, you know, we were supposed to be given a briefing on how to administer the Iowa tests. Instead, we were treated like children!"

"Children!" Ted laughed.

"Ted, it wasn't funny," Elaine chided. "We were treated like a bunch of illiterates—a bunch of morons! You know what it was like? It was like when you were in first grade and started to read!"

"What do you mean?" Ted asked, somewhat startled.

"Well, Mrs. Devor, the head of the guidance department, got up, and she decided she was going to lecture us on the tests. Okay so far, but instead of giving us an explanation, she asked us to follow along in the booklets they had passed out. This wouldn't have been half bad if she read us the instructions meant for the teachers, though we were quite capable of reading them ourselves. But, wait! That poor creature had the—the—I don't know what to call it—to read to us, *word by word*, the very instructions that we were to read to the *children*."

"Wow!"

"To top it off," Elaine continued, "she asked us to rewrite in the margin the very same material that was in the bold type in the booklet! Now, I ask you!"

"What in the world possessed this Mrs. Devor?" Ted queried.

"Ted, it's possible that I could have accepted this whole stupid thing, but it seems to me as if these guidance people want to feel important. They certainly were pushing us this morning."

Role-playing suggestions

[1]

CHARACTERS	SITUATION
ELAINE ROPER, *teacher-protagonist* TED ZEIS, *teacher* KATHY MAYER, *teacher* JOE ALPORT, *teacher*	During a coffee break later that day, Roper, Zeis, Mayer, and Alport discuss "Devor's meeting." Roper and Zeis are upset, while Alport thought the meeting was "rather well handled" and "necessary."

[2]

ELAINE ROPER HELEN DEVOR, *head of guidance*	Six months after the case incident, Devor asks Roper to help administer the Kuder Preference Record. Roper discusses her feelings openly with Devor.

Issue leads

The timing of meetings with teachers.

Teachers' role in testing programs.

Guidance counselors' role in testing programs.

The advisability of reading test instructions, word by word.

Who's afraid of Marda's mother?

The music reached a feverish pitch. Although most of the students had a singular style, they managed to keep the same rhythm. Marda Lowelson and her partner danced over toward Steve Larkin, Marda's science teacher.

"Hi, Mr. Larkin! Nice dance, isn't it?"

"Yes, it is! You're a pretty good dancer, Marda, I must say."

"Thank you. I wish I was as good in science."

"So do I, Marda. So do I."

As the dancers moved toward the center of the dance floor and began the intricate gyrations of the newest step, Steve thought to himself: "These kids amaze me. They take on a new personality outside the classroom." Marda was in Steve's advanced science class and was almost failing. Even though her record seemed to indicate that she was "bright," she wasn't producing. She became extremely excited during the tests and often said that she "forgot everything." And she never volunteered in class. Steve figured that she was too afraid to answer; afraid of being wrong. He had tried during all of the first quarter to encourage and support her, but without success.

Marda herself acutely felt the pressure, and she went to discuss her problem with Mr. Rankin, her guidance counselor. She asked if she could "please" get into the regular science class, but Rankin hedged. He said he couldn't do anything until he heard from Marda's parents. Right after that, Steve went to Don Rankin and recommended that Marda be dropped from his advanced class. "Most of the kids in there are whizzes, Don," he said. "I'm certain that

52

Marda could 'find' herself in regular science." Don Rankin said he would know more about what could be done after he had talked to Mr. and Mrs. Lowelson.

Steve thought of how rarely he had asked the guidance people for help. Yet, when a parent was coming in and there was some trouble brewing with one of the counselor's charges, the counselor wanted all the information and help he could get from Steve. And when guidance gave its tests each autumn, they wanted the teachers to help. "You'd think Don Rankin would be glad to reciprocate in some way," he thought. He realized that the counselors were busy with all the scheduling, program changes, and getting the students channeled into the "right" courses. Yet Steve wondered why much of this scheduling couldn't be taken care of by reasonably competent clerks instead of "high-priced" guidance counselors. What would the counselors do if that happened?

It seemed to him that the students hardly visited guidance for anything other than scheduling problems. He also wondered why Rankin wasn't more supportive with this problem. He knew that as long as district policy was such that the parent had so much say about the placement of his youngster, the counselor was limited in what he could do, but Steve felt certain counselors were more forceful and convincing with the parents than others. He wondered why certain counselors were able to support the teachers' recommendation if the teacher, in his best professional judgment, felt strongly about the placement of the student, while others seemed afraid of the parent. Others, like Don Rankin! With Don, the only way you could get a "misplaced" student out of a special class, once he was in, was to convince the parent yourself. No support from Rankin. And usually the only way you could convince the parent without the counselor's support was to see to it that the student failed at the end of the year. If the student ever managed to "just get by," then behold, he continued in the program. The advanced program was a kind of status symbol to many of the parents.

He thought of Myra Ferguson, one of the other counselors, and how helpful she had been with situations similar to this one. She really felt for the kids and stood up to their parents. Myra wasn't afraid! Steve thought that she felt as he did; that certain situations require a change. And furthermore, she would make a noble effort to effect the change, when she believed in it, parent or no! Even if no change came about, you felt that she was trying to help and was more on the side of the teacher than the parent.

Steve walked across the dance floor to where the group of chaperones were standing. He called Don Rankin aside and asked him if there had been any follow-up on his recommendation regarding the Lowelson girl.

"Well, Steve, I did speak to her mother. As you know, she's an officer in the PTA and very status conscious about having Marda in the advanced science class. I wish she would follow your recommendation, but . . ."

Role-playing suggestions

[1]

CHARACTERS	SITUATION
STEVE LARKIN, *teacher-protagonist* DON RANKIN, *guidance counselor* MYRA FERGUSON, *guidance counselor*	The day after the dance, Larkin meets with Rankin to discuss "the Lowelson case." Ferguson, standing nearby, suggests that Rankin reconsider his decision. Rankin takes exception.

[2]

STEVE LARKIN ANN KRAFT, *department head* PATRICIA BUTTEL, *teacher* BILL HELMSLEY, *teacher*	At a department meeting, Larkin says, "Guidance is afraid of parents." The others react, each a bit differently.

Issue leads

Guidance's specific role in scheduling students for various subjects.

Need for guidance to reciprocate for the help of the teacher.

Guidance counselors' fear of influential parents.

A surprise

One thing about Al Moore: he's an honest person. Not that the other counselors are dishonest. It's just that somehow I can't get to trust someone who walks around smiling all the time. When Al Moore has a problem, you can tell it by looking at his face. I used to really respect him. The reason I say "used to" is because of what happened in his office yesterday. I don't really dislike him because of what happened, but I certainly don't respect him for it. I like him, but I don't respect him. Follow?

Look, I don't want you to get the wrong idea. Fundamentally, I believe in the guidance approach. But yesterday's little incident makes me wonder about the qualifications of Al Moore as a counselor. He really put another teacher and me in a very awkward position, and I think he was insensitive to a new student's feelings too. You might understand the incident better if you picture doctors instead of teachers. Imagine a surgeon and two diagnosticians trying to discuss the complex diagnosis of an anxious patient while the patient looks on! It shouldn't happen! But it happened just like that right here at Berkly High School. Al Moore put Paul Merison and me in that very position.

Paul Merison is the other math teacher here at Berkly. He teaches the fast-track math, the college-prep type, and I teach the slower math. The slow math is a non-college course.

Yesterday morning, a new 10th-grader and her guardian aunt arrived at the guidance office to enroll at Berkly High. Paul Merison and I were called to Al Moore's office during our "preparation" period. This was customary. Whenever a new student comes to

Berkly and there is any question about his placement, the teachers are called in for their recommendation. That's why I really respect the guidance department here. That is, for the most part. I respect the counselors because they ask the teacher for advice. They don't set themselves up as experts in everything. If there is a problem about math, they ask a math teacher. If there is a problem about French, they ask a French teacher. But things seem to be changing. Counselors change. I've changed.

Funny how your views change as you mature. Six years ago, when I was just a high school senior, I thought the main business of guidance was to help get me into a college. My counselor really smiled when I came into the guidance office, because my grades and college boards were good and it wouldn't be too difficult to get me placed. I recall one time when he put up a big chart showing all of my class's board scores. Obviously, he wanted to foster competition. I thought it was a great idea then, but now, as a teacher of many of the slower kids, I would earnestly resent such a display.

Anyway, Paul and I were in Al Moore's office to make a placement recommendation. Paul and I customarily interview the student and have him work out a few problems. Then, shortly afterwards, we make a placement recommendation to Al Moore, who presents our recommendation to the child and the parent. Sounds efficient, doesn't it? Well, it is. That is, it was, until yesterday.

We were all sitting in the counselor's office—Al Moore, the student, her guardian aunt, Paul Merison, and I. The little girl said that she had a 76 average in math. We had no idea of what a 76 average meant in her previous school, and we couldn't figure out from the discussion just what math she had had. Unfortunately, the records don't ordinarily arrive until a month after the student.

The girl's aunt wanted her to take the college-prep math. We talked to the girl and had her work out a few algebra problems. You could see that she had some acquaintance with the problems but little competency. In our school we use a Euclidian method whereby you take step, defense, step, defense. Her previous teacher apparently was using some other method. It was really very difficult to figure the proper placement.

Now, here is the painful part. With all eyes on Paul and me, Al Moore said, "Well, gentlemen, you've seen what the young lady can do. Can we now have your decision, please?" I can't properly describe the tone of his voice, but believe me, he wanted us to answer him then and there. Everyone was staring at us, waiting for a decision. First, there was this terrible silence, and afterward the only sound you could hear was the movement of the chairs. The girl was squirming, and so were Paul and I.

Paul and I looked at each other. Who was going to answer? If I suggested the college-prep math, Paul might think I was pushing this new girl into his class. By the same token, Paul couldn't speak. There was so much that we needed to discuss. It was terribly frustrating and undignified for everyone, especially the girl. As I said, I've lost some respect.

Role-playing suggestions

[1]

CHARACTERS	SITUATION
DAVE FULLER, *teacher-protagonist* PAUL MERISON, *teacher* SELMA PROCTOR, *teacher*	During an informal occasion, Fuller describes the "awkward" situation that he and Merison were put into by Al Moore. Proctor finds Moore's behavior "indefensible."

[2]

DAVE FULLER AL MOORE, *guidance counselor* FRANCIS CLAYTON, *head of guidance*	Fuller discusses the "awkward" situation with Moore and Clayton. Moore is surprised.

Issue leads

The extent to which guidance counselors are looked upon as exemplars of model human relations.

Guidance's role in curriculum development.

The advantages of a counselor's drawing on a teacher's expertise in his subject specialty.

case **13**

Professional respect

Coach Arnie Sloan's hopes for his baseball team to improve on last year's record were diminishing. Tony Bixby, his best pitcher, was in academic trouble. He knew Tony wasn't a great student, but Arnie was shocked when Tony's father called him the previous night regarding the warnings Tony had just received in English, math, and science. And each of the teachers noted that Tony should have been coming for help after school. Arnie wished that he had known about Tony's predicament before this. It was much too late to do anything about it now.

Arnie had reported early to school the next morning, and the more he thought about the phone call from Tony's dad the previous evening, the more he fumed. He was pleased to find Pat LaGrande, the boys' physical education department head and Arnie's "boss," already in the physical education office. "It's times like this that a fellow needs a department head to talk to!" he thought. "I've a lot to get off my chest."

He told Pat about his star pitcher. "Why, Arnie," Pat said, "you mean Tony's guidance counselor, Adele Caldwell, didn't give you any clue that Tony was getting in trouble upstairs?"

"No!"

"Well, Arnie, the guidance people are overburdened."

Intermittently, throughout the day, between classes and mutual "free periods" Arnie and Pat talked about guidance.

"Pat, they do this to us all the time. Guidance never, or almost never, comes to us until it's too late. Tony's father tells me that Adele Caldwell's been involved with Tony all year and especially

58

this quarter. The guidance people don't share what they know with the other teachers."

"This time they didn't come at all, did they?"

"No, they didn't. Sometimes I've gone to guidance and said, what's the story on so and so, and they'd say, oh, yeah, we're having a great deal of difficulty with him, and it revolves around this problem and that problem. But this could have gone for a year and I'd never know. Like Tony. He's been an angel down here. Kids are pretty good at covering up. They can do that relatively easy in physical education. Guidance never once came to me this entire year and asked me for information."

"Sometimes they sent those yellow sheets around about the kids, remember?"

"Yes, but you know as well as I do that those questionnaires are impersonal and very sparse. They don't get down to the heart of the kid. The counselor should meet with us and discuss the kids with us. We've got lots of information that isn't available anywhere else. We observe kids that are withdrawn, the youngster who has a lot of fears about gym, and all of the problems that go along with going to gym, the youngster who's afraid of physical contact, the one who's reticent about getting undressed in front of other kids. Lots of these things. If they think we're professionals and we think they're professionals, they'll come to us on a professional level. As well as giving information, we'd like to get some. It's too bad we can't make case conferences, but we have sports after school. Guidance doesn't have to divulge many of the secrets and many of the problems that the youngster has confided in them, but certainly they can let us know that this is a kid who may need a little extra. They seldom do.

"If a mother comes into guidance and says, 'My Jimmy doesn't have any friends,' this is what we should know right away. Right, Pat?"

"Right!"

"We say to the kid, 'Hey! Come on out for intramurals this afternoon!' Or, 'Why don't you go out for this team?'—if he has ability that way. Our subject lends itself to a great deal of influence."

"That's another thing," said Pat. "I wonder how much influence the counselors have with the kids."

"I don't think many of the kids go to their counselor voluntarily.

Most of them are called down. I've heard this from kids. They're very reluctant to walk in. Most children do need someone to listen to them, but guidance can't expect to sit in their offices and wait for people to come just because a counselor goes to a class and says, 'If you have a problem, come and see me!' It's a great stigma for the kid to say to a teacher, 'Where's the guidance office? I want to see Mrs. Caldwell.' Kids are afraid to do that. So the only ones that go on their own are the kids with the gumption and guts to go on their own. A lot of kids are walking around with their problems and will continue to walk around with them. In essence, what I'm saying is that the guidance counselor has to get out and draw these kids in, or they'll never come."

"But how would he draw them in?" Pat asked.

"He's got to be much more gregarious than the counselors are. The counselor has to be a pusher. He's got to go to the musicals and observe which of his kids are there. He would observe that four of his kids are in the brass section, and two are in the winds, and three are in the chorus. He won't remember all of them, of course. But when he sees one of the kids he says, 'Hey, John, you did a nice job with your trumpet! Your solo was just sensational!' That's enough to open the door. He has to go to athletic contests. He has to go to the art department and see whose painting is on the wall. He might pick up nine kids there. He should go to print shop and see who is doing well. He may pick up a few more. Then there's the wood shop, and so on.

"He should know which of his kids are class officers. He should get to know these kids as individuals. He must take an interest in them. The kid doesn't know that all you did was see that he played the trumpet in the band. He thinks the counselor knows where he lives, his mother, his uncle, and he thinks the counselor knows a lot about him. I think that then the student would be more apt to go to the counselor when a problem comes up. He'd feel that the counselor knew him. But unfortunately, the counselors hardly ever come to intramurals or athletic events."

"One thing about teaching physical education, Arnie, we've no trouble getting most of the boys to come to us."

"Years ago, before we had all these counselors, many more academic teachers came to us to help with kids. Now guidance has intercepted many of these referrals and is doing little or no lateraling, so to speak. Now the teacher tells guidance, gets the problem off his chest, and that's where it seems to end. The guidance people don't take advantage of what we have to offer. Also, they seem to schedule conferences with kids indiscriminately during gym periods. Does guidance take kids out of physical education because guidance doesn't think physical education is important?"

Then something ironic happened. Tony Bixby, Arnie's "failing" pitcher, came to Coach Arnie Sloan at the beginning of class. "Coach," he said, "I've received this pass to go to guidance instead of gym class this period. Will you sign it so I can go?"

Role-playing suggestions

[1]

CHARACTERS

ARNIE SLOAN, *teacher-protagonist*
PAT LA GRANDE, *department head*
BARBARA COLLINS, *mathematics teacher*

SITUATION

During an informal occasion, Sloan, LaGrande, and Collins discuss the relative virtues of the "academics" and "phys ed." Collins speaks disparagingly of "phys ed" and Sloan talks about the need for more "professional respect."

[2]

ARNIE SLOAN
LEFTY FAUST, *student and baseball player*
SHORTIE WILSON, *student and baseball palyer*
TERRY BRANCA, *student and baseball player*

Faust, Wilson and Branca, upset because of Tony Bixby's ineligibility, request an explanation. After hearing Sloan's explanation, one of the students speaks disparagingly of guidance. Sloan reacts in character.

Issue leads

Difficulties encountered by guidance counselors and "phys ed" teachers in trying to share information about certain students.

The effectiveness of questionnaires regarding student behavior.

The physical education teacher's special influence upon certain students.

The counselors' problem in "attracting" counselees.

Make no waves

"Well, Drew, how do you like it at Glenside?" asked Alec Carpenter, the head counselor at Summerton.

Drew Flesher had been a social studies teacher at Summerton High for five years before going to Glenside Junior High. Drew always liked it at Summerton, but he was lured to Glenside by the combination of a sizable salary increase and the prospect of a more cosmopolitan life, since Glenside was part of a large metropolitan area.

It was summer, and Drew had just finished his first full year at Glenside. He was back in Summerton, trying to recapture some of his recent past. He made a visit to his old school and, by chance, found Al Carpenter in the guidance suite. Almost everyone else was away for the summer vacation.

"Well, Carp, it's certainly not anything like Summerton! To be honest with you, the entire atmosphere is different. I didn't realize how well off the teacher was, here at Summerton. You don't have to compete with your neighbors as much, and the teacher holds a much better place in the community. There's also more respect for the school itself here. I haven't forgotten how the whole community would turn out just for a basketball game. It was an event. Carp, the teachers—and the guidance people too—are more devoted here."

"What is the guidance department like at Glenside, Drew?"

"Well, I remember how if we had a problem with a student here, we really worked together to solve it. If a teacher walked into this office with a problem, you fellows welcomed him. When I walk in with a problem at Glenside, I get a 'Why? What are you bothering me for?" At least, that's the attitude I feel. And I've heard it repeated by many of the older teachers too. I'm at the point now where I just don't refer anyone. I'm involved in an especially sad situation with guidance right now."

"What's that?"

"Toward the end of each academic year at Glenside, all the teachers of a certain section have a meeting with the counselors and other specialists. You see, at Glenside we have certain groups in the junior high that all have the same teachers. They move about in groups. So last week, just before the end of school, we had this sectional meeting. Ordinarily, lots of good can come from this kind of meeting, but listen.

"One of my students, a girl by the name of May Warten, was being discussed. A name would come up, and then the different teachers that had her would make comments. Then we would compare and the counselor would make notes. If guidance seemed in order, fine! The nurse was there, and so was the reading consultant.

"We ran through the names of the students in the remedial group. At Glenside we have three levels: remedial, for the slow students; regular; and honors. The remedial group isn't a true remedial group either. Most of the students in there aren't achieving because they misbehave. My idea of a true remedial student is one who is a slow learner but who wants to learn.

"This particular girl was not a remedial-type student. She was a bright girl, a mature girl, a pretty girl, and a well-behaved girl. By virtue of being in this class, she had aligned herself with a number of the discipline problems in the school and really lost interest in her studies. All of the teachers felt the same way about her and said that she shouldn't continue in that class. All of this was recorded by the counselor, but the philosophy at Glenside is: 'Make no waves.' "

"What's going to happen to this youngster?"

"I think you'll understand better if I tell you about another incident that shows how they operate at Glenside. Earlier this year, a mother called me regarding her son, who was in my American history class. It got complicated, so I said, 'Look, let me speak to your son's guidance counselor.' I thought that I could sit down with the counselor and look into the boy's problem. When I mentioned the problem to the counselor, he laughed. That's right. He laughed. He said, 'What can be done about it? That's the way this boy is!' I said, 'Look, does that go for the record now? At least I've told you!' He shook his head and laughed and walked away. I got this more than once, and so did some of the other teachers. And it wasn't just one counselor.

"Apathy seems to permeate the whole school. Guidance, like teaching, is run by school policy, and the policy at Glenside seems to be, 'Make no waves. No matter what, don't rock the boat.' As long as you don't have any ostensible discipline problems, all is well.

"In discussing the counselors, some of the older teachers have said, 'They're good boys, but their hands are tied too.' You know, the funny thing is that I like each of the counselors personally. But my opinion is that they're in it primarily for the 'goof-off' time and the extra money. Some of them weren't too happy with their subject area when they were teaching.

"But, Carp, your co-worker, Florence, is just the opposite of this. She's one of the most devoted counselors that anyone could ever know."

"Yes, she can find a spark of good in every child."

"And she's admired for it. She has my respect, I'll say that much. But you know—off the cuff—here and there, some of the staff felt that she was overly interested in the kids."

"Better that way than the way you've described at Glenside, eh, Drew?"

"Yes, indeed. She's a very understanding person. Her way of thinking is the right one for a guidance counselor. You don't mind the paperwork and meetings when you feel that the counselor is devoted."

"Well, what was the final outcome of the sectional conference regarding May Warten?"

"This was an extreme case, where something should have been done. A mere flick of the program could put May from the remedial class into the regular class and would do wonders for her. But, of course, no change was made. At least nothing was contemplated when I left last week, even though all the teachers said it was the thing to do. We'll lose that girl for sure if she stays in remedial. Carp, do you think I should continue to fight for her being changed this summer or even next year, when school resumes?"

Role-playing suggestions

[1]

CHARACTERS

DREW FLESHER, *teacher protagonist*
SAM HENNESEY, *guidance counselor*
MRS. WARTEN, *parent*
MAY WARTEN, *student*

SITUATION

A year after the case situation, Mrs. Warten asks Hennesey permission for her daughter to be placed in a "higher track." Hennesey refuses.

[2]

DREW FLESHER
PROFESSOR CRAIG, *counselor educator*
DOMINIC KEVIN, *graduate student*
LOIS VOLVA, *graduate student*

Attending a course in guidance, Flesher is asked by Craig for his "description of the counselor's role." Kevin and Volva participate in the discussion that emanates from Flesher's "description."

Issue leads

Advantages of group meetings regarding whole sections of students.

When a counselor should "make waves."

When a teacher should "make waves."

Fresh fish

"All right, who's the wise guy that put this sticker on my locker?"

"Don't look now, John, but there's that boy again!"

"It's Henry Barna, the sticker man! It's a bird; it's a plane; it's a sticker man!" yelped three girls.

Mrs. Keith, teacher of Social Living I, stepped out into the hall. "What's all this rumpus here? Oh, it's you, Henry Barna, creating trouble again. Put those fish stickers away!"

Henry drew back, then turned and skipped down the corridor, hooting and flailing at an invisible army of attacking Mrs. Keiths.

A slow anger seethed through Mrs. Keith's system. She asked herself, "How could he have had the nerve? That boy is impossible!" All over the blackboard were pasted dozens of Henry's fish stickers. "Fresh Fish Every Friday," they read. Mrs. Keith quickly decided that they were hijacked from O'Connor's Market. She then noticed, somewhat resignedly and with a wry smile, that more stickers were pasted on the desk and files. "God, the boy's really cut loose today," she thought.

According to Lucille Keith, Henry Barna was impossible to describe. Indeed, Henry was an obvious hazard in the halls, the cafeteria, the gym, the street, and, of course, in Social Living I. Believe it or not, Henry's mother had to pay him to come to school. His was an exciting household. Often, when Henry wouldn't settle down quickly enough to do his homework, his father would throw a chair or two at him. All kinds of weird things went on in his life. Naturally, Henry often interrupted Mrs. Keith's lectures by calling out unconnected comments. His classmates ridiculed him, but Henry enjoyed the attention, though perhaps it wasn't exactly of an affectionate nature.

Mrs. Keith was bewildered by Henry's actions. It was only her second year of teaching, even though she was approaching forty. She had attended evening classes in education for almost a half dozen years, all the while raising a family and pleasing her husband. One of her two children was retarded, and she felt a great compassion for all children and their parents. But Henry Barna—heavens!

The guidance department told Mrs. Keith to try to "guide" as many students as she could during homeroom, but she felt extremely inept in the realm of guidance. "Call on us whenever you need some help," guidance said. Then when she called for help so often, they said they just didn't have the personnel or time to serve her. But the counselors were very nice and worked hard. "They need understanding more than anyone else," thought Mrs. Keith.

It was obvious that Henry needed help in Social Living I, because he just couldn't contain himself. After the fish sticker incident, Mrs. Keith ran to Henry's friendly guidance counselor. "He's a menace, Mr. Lampman!" she declared. She told Mr. Lampman all about Henry and especially about the fish stickers. "He's really a very *disturbed* lad and needs a psychiatrist!" she concluded.

"Wait a minute, Mrs. Keith," Lampman warned. "Don't get carried away! You're not really qualified to put psychological labels on a student. Nor am I, for that matter. To attempt to render a diagnosis without proper psychological training puts one on untenable ground! What right have you, my dear Mrs. Keith, to make such assumptions?"

Mrs. Keith meekly responded, "Gee whiz, none, I guess."

Mrs. Keith once had another problem with another boy who was too slow for her regular class. She recommended to guidance that the boy be transferred to her weaker class and explained that the boy, fortunately, had a study period that met at the same time as the weaker class. Guidance accepted and wished to act upon her recommendation, but the principal didn't. Naturally, guidance didn't want to "buck" the administration, so Mrs. Keith secretly transferred the boy on her own. After the change proved workable, she enlisted her department head's support, and the change was given de facto approval by the powers. "Sometimes a teacher just has to take things into her own hands," Mrs. Keith believed, but she went along with Lampman's attitude about "assumptions" regarding psychological diagnoses. "I'll wait," she thought. Lampman had arranged for Henry Barna to be "objectively tested" by The Bureau of Psychological Services.

Weeks went by. Henry continued his obstreperous ways. Mrs. Keith continued to be bewildered and exasperated. Finally Mr. Lampman called Mrs. Keith to his office. "Mrs. Keith," Lampman began in a low, grim voice, "the psychologist has completed a psychological analysis of Henry Barna, the young man in your Social Living I class."

"Oh, yes, I recall the youngster," said Mrs. Keith politely.

"Well, he's been carefully tested. The confidential diagnosis indicated rather conclusively that he has a very nebulous self-picture, based primarily upon a non-supportive relationship with his father."

"Hmm, very interesting," said Mrs. Keith.

"Mrs. Keith, I'm sorry to state this, but I think you should know. Henry Barna couldn't even control himself sufficiently to put the x's in the little boxes on the test sheet!"

"Goodness," said Mrs. Keith.

"I'm afraid he's a very disturbed boy, Mrs. Keith."

"I'm sorry to hear that," said Mrs. Keith as she scratched at the fish sticker that someone had affixed to the front of Mr. Lampman's desk.

Role-playing suggestions

[1]

CHARACTERS	SITUATION
LUCILLE KEITH, *teacher-protagonist* ARNOLD DAVISON, *teacher* RONALD SLAGG, *teacher* NAOMI PETERSEN, *teacher*	At an informal occasion, Keith describes her problems with Henry Barna. Slagg feels that Keith should have refused to allow Barna to continue in class until guidance had provided "something concrete" in the form of help. Keith reacts in character.

[2]

LUCILLE KEITH

HENRY BARNA, *student*

After school, Barna describes
what "the head shrinker" did.
Keith tries to "reach" the boy
with advice.

Issue leads

The different character of teachers' vs.
counselors' relationships with problem students.

Guidance's offer to help, without the available personnel
to follow through.

Teacher's qualification to pronounce a student "disturbed."

When guidance should "buck" the administration.

When teachers should "buck" the administration.

To each his own

Each of the guidance counselors here at Madison is quite different. Ginny Sherman is the efficiency expert. She gives you exactly and precisely what you ask for and that's it. Although Oscar Pennington is a kind of simple fellow, he's all for the kids. In fact, he's a regular male Pollyanna. That can be a little sickening after a while. Then there's Miss Alice Vander. Let me tell you about Miss Vander.

I found a few precious minutes before my fifth period Spanish class a couple of days ago, so I hustled on down to the guidance office to get some background information on Craig Richards. Craig is a senior who's failing Spanish II—I believe for the second time! I never did find out the full story about his background in Spanish. That's because I made the *mistake* of asking Miss Vander about Craig.

Maybe I'd better clue you in on the kind of pressures we language teachers must contend with at Madison before I go any further. Then you'll understand why the information I was after was so important. You see, many students here are pressed into taking a foreign language, whether they have an aptitude for it or not. Then the least capable ones always seem to take Spanish, because for some reason there's a widespread myth that Spanish is the easiest language. Here on the Coast, it seems that people are crawling all over each other trying to get ahead. There's panic over grades and college, and every child is pressed to aim for the "highest horizons." My feeling is, if a child isn't able, and doesn't really need Spanish in the vocation toward which he is aiming, then he should not continue suffering with it. Why should his parents be allowed to *force* him to take it? Colleges? Not all colleges, the counselors tell me, require a language. These students, if they really want college, should apply to the colleges that don't require languages. That's all!

Believe me, it's quite disheartening to look out and see the very sad and defeated faces of some of these children, especially when most of the class is progressing beautifully. It seems kind of sadistic, doesn't it?

Well, Craig Richards seemed to be in this defeated category, and I thought it might be most insightful for me to know more about his I.Q., his previous grades in English and Spanish, and whether he ever took another language. Things like that.

I was about to go to Craig's file when Alice Vander spotted me from her little booth. "Welcome to guidance, Cora. I'm *so* glad when a teacher is *truly* interested in her students." (As if a teacher couldn't be "truly interested in her students" without coming to guidance!) "Craig Richards; oh, yes! A very handsome boy. Cora, I've heard that his father is a very heavy drinker. I believe that Mr. Richards has been quite sick emotionally as well. Mrs. Richards has called me on the phone several times this year, and I think that she has had to take over all of the responsibilities of managing the home *and* Craig. Mrs. Richards, I've heard, has never had a really good relationship with her husband. You can imagine the effect that all this has had on Craig." And on and on and on, to the point where if the bell for the fifth period didn't ring, I would have left anyhow!

Now maybe I shouldn't be too hard on Miss Vander. I'm sure that she means well, and old wives' tales are just part of her nature. It all boils down, mostly, to the fact that I don't want to be a time-waster. It's *my* nature.

Now, my kind of counselor (you've guessed it) is Ginny Sherman. She gives you exactly and precisely what you want. Tell her your problem and one, two, three, she's taken the necessary steps. She culls the required information from the cumulative record; she contacts and sees the parents and the student, if appropriate; and then, without delay, she invites the teacher back and has precisely what the teacher needs. That's my kind of guidance counselor!

Role-playing suggestions

[1]

CHARACTERS

OSCAR PENNINGTON, *guidance counselor*
ALICE VANDER, *guidance counselor*
GINNY SHERMAN, *guidance counselor*

SITUATION

These three persons each have a different point of view as to the kinds of services they would like guidance to provide. They have a lively discussion.

[2]

CORA MAYO, *teacher-protagonist*
CLARA LASSER, *teacher*
CECILIA DAWN, *teacher*

Mayo describes to Lasser and Dawn her problems with Miss Vander. They are surprised, because Miss Vander has such a "good reputation with the kids."

Issue leads

The need for a counselor to be aware of the individual differences of teachers.

The intrusion of the time factor on a teacher's guidance role.

Pressures peculiar to language teachers.

How to be truly interested in a student without using the guidance facility.

Sensing what a teacher wants from guidance.

Coping with Alvin Slade

School policy dictated that Hilda Cronston, the French teacher, secure the approval of a child's guidance counselor before being allowed to drop a child from her French course. For more than a week, she had been totally unsuccessful in her attempts to meet with Mr. Charlie Tyler, guidance counselor. She wanted Alvin Slade dropped from French right away.

Mr. Tyler never seemed to be in his office during Hilda Cronston's available periods. Hilda observed: "He's either having his lunch, in an 'important' conference with a parent or student, or at a meeting. It's getting slightly ridiculous, trying to get a few words with this guy. He's harder to see than the principal."

Weeks before, Hilda had had a conference with Alvin Slade's mother. She explained to Mrs. Slade that Alvin's very poor showing in French that whole first term had put him in a difficult position. "If a youngster gets off to a poor start in a foreign language, Mrs. Slade, it is more serious than in many other subjects. In a language you must rely and build upon previous knowledge. Unfortunately, Alvin has no foundation now to build upon."

Mrs. Slade had nodded her understanding dejectedly. Then she said, "I guess I'd better speak with Alvin's guidance counselor and see what he thinks we should do."

"All right, if you wish," Hilda responded. She wondered, "What on earth could Charlie Tyler offer Mrs. Slade that I haven't already given? The boy hasn't worked yet, and even if he started to work at this late date, it doesn't seem possible for him to make up what he has lost." Hilda had heard Charlie Tyler comment about parents while lounging in the faculty room. "Mrs. So-and-so is coming in. I'll be damned if I know what to tell her. Who can tell a parent that her kid is stupid?" Hilda thought then, "What a great shame that these parents think if they see guidance, they're actually accomplishing something. It's so deceitful—but when a child is failing, I guess seeing the counselor appeases their guilt feelings."

Hilda's mind returned to the present. "Alvin Slade is going backward in French. He knows almost nothing." Hilda could sense his great embarrassment when she called on him in class and he didn't know how to answer. Recently he had been turning to horseplay. "He's really become a disturbance to the whole class, as well as to himself," she thought.

Hilda's only alternative was to wait until after school to see Charlie Tyler, and this choice she abhorred. Language people always had a big turnout for extra help. She would have to cancel the help session and wait down in "that" guidance office until she could see Charlie Tyler about dropping Alvin Slade. "Oh, how much better it would be," she thought, "if there were a regularly scheduled meeting with guidance every so often to review the various students' performances and get these drop approvals without all of this chasing around." Hilda had never, in her four years of teaching, even met with a counselor to get additional background information about her students. She wondered why she hadn't. She wasn't really sure that the counselors would be willing or, if willing, would have anything substantial to offer. But she wondered why they never conferred anyway. Wasn't that part of their job?

Finally, after school, Hilda did get to see Mr. Charlie Tyler. Tyler explained, "Alvin Slade's aptitude tests show that he has the potential, and therefore he has the right to stay in French and fail— if he and his parents want him to." Hilda couldn't understand the logic of Charlie's statement, but she decided that she wasn't going to worry any further. Alvin would stay in French.

Upon leaving the counselor's office, Hilda Cronston thought, "When things go wrong for a student today, the first place he runs is to his guidance counselor—and there are always such lines."

When Hilda first came to work in the public schools, she was "shocked" at the way students "ran" to guidance. "I hope guidance is helping them, but I don't see how. I didn't have this kind of guidance when I was in school. I learned to solve my own problems."

Hilda shuddered when she thought of continuing to try to deal with Alvin Slade's horseplay in French class. "That was good training for me—solving my own problems! That training will come in handy when I cope with Alvin Slade."

Role-playing suggestions

[1]

CHARACTERS	SITUATION
HILDA CRONSTON, *teacher-protagonist*	At a conference, Cronston explains to Slade that he may very well fail French. After Slade leaves, Cronston tells Tyler how she feels about guidance.
CHARLIE TYLER, *guidance counselor*	
ALVIN SLADE, *student*	

[2]

HILDA CRONSTON	A year after the case incident, at an informal occasion, Cronston describes to the other teachers how Slade failed French. Forest is "dismayed" at the way guidance handled the case. Cronston asks, "Well, what could guidance have been expected to do anyway?"
MARTHA FOREST, *beginning teacher*	
LEE CHILDS, *teacher*	
STAN HAUSER, *teacher*	

Issue leads

How a counselor can become more accessible to teachers.

Offhand comments in the faculty room.

Advisability of teachers and guidance counselors meeting on a regular basis.

A student's "right" to fail if he chooses.

When guidance "overprotects" students.

Buzzers and bells
It was Archie Fleming's chance to get a quick cup of coffee. Seated at one side of the faculty room were Dan Cullen and Sam Carnegie, guidance counselors, having "another" coffee break.

Archie couldn't help overhearing the enthusiasm and excitement in Sam's voice as he talked with Dan Cullen about his group counseling sessions. As Archie carried his coffee over to Agnes Perrin, a teaching colleague, he said softly to her, "Agnes, those counselors seem to be drinking coffee here in the faculty room as much as anything else. By the way, have you noticed how Sam Carnegie has changed ever since he got back from that guidance institute at Harnell U. last year?"

"Yes," Agnes said. "He's been just chock full of enthusiasm for his guidance."

"They moved in too fast with this guidance here at Knightsbridge. They went overboard, I think. Guidance was supposed to be the savior; it was going to save everything. Four counselors for only six hundred students. That's been some deal for those counselors!"

"And as their workload decreased, ours got heavier!"

"They went off to big schools and came back with a lot of big ideas," Archie continued, "but they're in their own world. They haven't even tried to educate us, the students, or the parents as to what they're doing. They're on one side of the fence, and we're on the other.

"You know, I've made my share of referrals to their office, but do you think there was any follow-up? Oh, they'd talk to the youngster, but they never once told me what I, as a teacher, should or could do or, for that matter, what they've accomplished with the referral."

R-r-ring went the inevitable bell. Archie and Agnes carried their cups to the sink and left the room. Over their shoulder they couldn't help but notice that the two counselors were still engrossed in their coffee and discussion, even though the next class was about to start.

Archie was looking forward to this particular English class. He had, for the last few weeks, been carefully building the concept that he expected to clinch today. He was going to use T. S. Eliot's "The Hollow Men" to demonstrate that, as he put it, "the emotion of great poetry is absolutely impersonal"—that "the emotion has its life in the poem and not in the history of the poet."

As he poured himself into his oral reading of "The Hollow Men," he could sense the excitement of his class. "They're on the brink of a marvelous insight," he thought. "This is teaching! Building to this wonderful moment when suddenly the student is able to see all of the bits and pieces clink magnificently into perspective."

Archie was closing in on that moment. He was in grand voice and Eliot's lines were ringing true. "Between the desire and the spasm; between the potency and the—" Buzz, buzz. The loud ringing of a buzzer interrupted. He repeated. "Between the potency and the exist—" Buzz, buzz, buzz went the buzzer on the intercom.

Archie stopped. The letdown of the class was obvious. Tempo broken, Archie realized with great chagrin that that beautiful moment of insight would have to wait.

"Hello, Mr. Fleming, is that you?" said the voice over the intercom. "Hope I haven't interrupted anything."

"Oh, no; what can I do for you, please?"

"Mr. Fleming, is Giggi Dombar there?"

"Yes, she is."

"Could you possibly send her to the guidance office right away? Mr. Carnegie wants to see her. Or would the end of the period be more convenient?"

"I'll send her right down."

The spell broken, Archie limped through Eliot's masterpiece. "Insight, I hope you'll show up tomorrow!" he thought.

"Why don't they pull the students out of their own group guidance classes, or physical education, or health? At least if they let me in on what they're accomplishing, or if they gave me some good ideas on how to help when I refer someone, I could tolerate these damned buzzers and bells."

Role-playing suggestions

[1]

CHARACTERS	SITUATION
ARCHIE FLEMING, *teacher-protagonist* SAM CARNEGIE, *guidance counselor*	Fleming, in Carnegie's office, asks Carnegie why he wanted to see Giggi Dombar. Carnegie tries to explain why he called for the girl. Fleming reacts in character.

[2]

ARCHIE FLEMING AGNES PERRIN, *teacher* LOLA MC BEE, *teacher* TRACY HOBART, *teacher*	All are discussing guidance at an informal occasion. Fleming describes how he felt when his class was once interrupted (in case).

Issue leads

The value of a counselor conducting business "over coffee."

Procedures a counselor should follow in "feedback" to a teacher.

Prescription vs. diagnosis as a guidance service to teachers.

The effect upon a teacher of a class interruption.

Occasions when a counselee need be seen during class time.

Holy Angels

"Cathy McGrath is really in a traumatic state this year, Wally. You see, all of the McGraths' children except her are paragons of success. Cathy is the only one of their eight kids who wasn't able to make it in Holy Angels Parochial School and had to come to Cleveland High. This has undoubtedly had a devastating effect on her ego, Wally."

Wally couldn't see it. Cathy was a cooperative student in his homeroom; an enthusiastic participant in his Future Teachers of America Club; and was doing adequate work, with only a few exceptions, in his 10th-grade English class. "She's one of the happiest, most well-rounded, secure youngsters you'd ever want to meet," he thought as Gene Memphis, Cathy's guidance counselor, spoke. "These guidance counselors are always trying to probe too deeply into healthy kids and coming up with all kinds of tremendous problems I don't think really exist. Sure, Cathy can't spell, but where does all this personal background come into spelling?"

Memphis left the study hall, and Wally's mind stayed on guidance rather than on his supervision of the study. "I wish they'd stop getting into the moral life of the kids here. It may make for interesting conversation, but it rarely helps me in the classroom.

"Oh, certain kinds of things might be pertinent, such as a child's father is out of a job so that the child isn't eating or isn't dressed properly, or a mother is ill and a student has to spend much of her time taking care of the other young ones in the family. But not all those other probings. I believe the student, like all of us, is entitled to *some* privacy.

"There are paradoxes. The people who were counselors in the three schools in which I've worked were probably among the most impressive people that I have ever met in education. At Xavier, my first school, one gentleman had about ten years of classroom experience, was a full colonel in the army, had worked in industry, and had raised a good family of his own. Many of the others, in the public schools, had similarly impressive qualifications. Often they had worked with youngsters in sports. But even with these outstanding people, the guidance programs have been of little service to me. I think that the guidance departments operate under false flags. They claim to be a teacher *service*, but the teacher does most of the work. He fills out all their questionnaires on student behavior; he proctors and sometimes grades their tests; he writes up their student evaluation sheets at the end of the year.

"Now if I, as a teacher, wanted some special information on John Q., such as his I.Q. and reading scores, and I sent the guidance people a form to fill out, they'd say, 'Come down and check the folder!'

"So what happens? Data goes from the tests and the various teachers into the files. Then it's a dead end. If the teachers want to get at it, they have to take a lot of time and energy and go down to get it. Getting the information isn't as easy as it would seem on paper. The teacher has countless commitments to time during the school day.

"Now, I don't dispute that guidance has a lot of good, solid, and useful information lying dormant in its files. I predict that some day an enlightened guidance department will have a kind of I.B.M. card sent to each of a student's teachers. On that card, in some kind of code, will be condensed all of the pertinent and vital background information regarding a student: reading scores, I.Q.'s, other teachers' observations about the student's success and failures. The works. But no absurd, far-out psychological speculations like, 'Cathy McGrath can't spell because she's the only one in her family that didn't get into parochial school.'

"Also, regarding the psychological approaches of the counselor, a counselor should remember who he is and what his limitations are. He shouldn't forget that he is a faculty member first and foremost. A counselor shouldn't tolerate gross complaining about teachers by a student. When he receives these complaints, a counselor has an obligation to instruct the student and make him aware of what is expected. The counselor should support the teacher and explain that the teacher is more mature and has been around the bases once more than the kid. I think the student has the right to speak his mind, but only if he does it in a dignified and respectful way—not with all the tear shedding that seems to go on.

"Counselors should stick to facts and stick to the surface. Not 'This girl had a baby here,' and 'That girl had a baby there.' Some of that may be interesting and even factual, but it certainly isn't consequential in helping a teacher teach."

Wally turned his mind to a stack of ungraded spelling papers that he had pulled from his briefcase. Cathy McGrath's paper was on top of the stack. Wally smiled oddly when he noticed what Cathy had inadvertently doodled in the margin of her paper: "Holy Angels."

Role-playing suggestions

[1]

CHARACTERS	SITUATION
WALLY MARTIN, *teacher-protagonist* CATHY MC GRATH, *student*	After class Martin and McGrath discuss McGrath's feelings about not being admitted to Holy Angels. McGrath shows a lot of pent-up feeling.

[2]

WALLY MARTIN PAULA BATES, *teacher* DAVID EGAN, *teacher* BRUCE DUNHAM, *teacher*	Martin and other teachers discuss the propriety of guidance's probing into the personal life of students.

Issue leads

Whether a counselor should probe into a student's moral life.

Differences between teacher and counselor as to appropriate depth of investigation into students' problems.

case 20

No encouragement

"Tell me, Mr. Barlow, why didn't you refer the Hansen girl to the guidance department in the first place? You would have avoided this sticky predicament that you're in, you know. That's why we have a guidance department, Mr. Barlow."

Roscoe Barlow, a social studies teacher, responded, "I honestly would have, Dr. Hopkins, if I could have felt that the guidance people could have—or would have—done something positive. But, Dr. Hopkins, in the time that I've been here at Grant High School, I must confess, I've never been given any reason to suspect that the guidance department gets involved with the personal life of the students."

"Ye gads, man, where have you been? That's a key phase of our guidance counselor's work."

"Is it? I'm shocked. I know that that's the theory, but I don't think the practice here is that, is it? Dr. Hopkins, I know the counselor isn't a psychologist or psychiatrist, but he should be able to offer some insight to a teacher. Frankly, sir, I don't know what the counselors do. Maybe they do help the students on a personal basis, but I've never heard about it. I don't hear the kids say anything. You've never given me any orientation into what they're doing. As I said, if they're helping these youngsters with their personal and social problems, it's been a well-kept secret from me. Undoubtedly it's been happening if you say so, sir, but it's been happening behind closed doors."

"Roscoe, we like your teaching. We like the kind of work you've been doing, but you've overstepped once too often the bounds of your job. Frankly, I'm not certain, myself, exactly what my guidance department is up to all the time. But, Roscoe, you've got to know your own limits."

"Dr. Hopkins, as far as I'm concerned, that's the way it has been; the guidance department goes its way and I go mine. Listen, many of the other teachers here realize, as I do, that the guidance department must exist, but we've got no feeling for it one way or the other. Oh, once in a while they ask me if I would send a letter of recommendation to help someone get into college or get a job, but it seems their major function is the preparing and sending of transcripts and putting grades on records.

"You know, sir, in all the time I've been here at Grant, not once—not once—was I ever invited to meet with a counselor and talk about a student. It seems awfully funny that we don't have that kind of interaction. And it's a shame, because I have a lot of kids I can't get to—like the Hansen girl."

"Mr. Barlow, I think you're projecting too much of the blame for your predicament on our guidance department."

"Don't get me wrong, sir. They're wonderful people in that department, and I know they work very hard. Just the number of students they see each day suggests that. Even if they only said 'hello' to each one, they'd have to be working hard. But, sir, they give me no encouragement to use their offices. Shouldn't the initiative come from them?"

Role-playing suggestions

[1]

CHARACTERS	SITUATION
ROSCOE BARLOW, *teacher-protagonist* STAN CARSON, *head of guidance* DR. HOPKINS, *principal*	In Hopkins' office, Barlow, Carson, and Hopkins discuss the "role of guidance in our school." Hopkins is surprised when Carson reveals his ideas about the purposes of the guidance department.

[2]

ROSCOE BARLOW
CAROL HANSON, *student* (*in case*)
ALAN PARSONS, *student*

Hanson and Parsons are describing, in a negative manner, their contacts with their counselor. Barlow responds in character.

Issue leads

To what extent teachers should become involved with their charges.

To what extent counselors should become involved with their charges.

The difficulty of effectively communicating guidance's role to teachers.

Why certain teachers feel apathetic toward guidance.

Who should be responsible for promoting the use of guidance services.

A bad taste

"Charlie, I wouldn't care if she were Jehova," Paul declared. "She can't talk to me like that. I told her where she could get off. I went in and told her exactly how I felt, and she said, 'I don't care what you think. I'm the child's guidance counselor!'"

"Okay," Charlie said. "What happened?"

"Well, she asked me about a certain boy in my class, and I told her about the troubles he was causing, but I made it clear to her that I didn't want him out, because that is exactly what he wanted."

"And she took the child out anyway?"

"Correct! She disregarded everything I said. She had arranged to switch the boy to Helen Carden's class before I had even spoken with him."

"Helen Carden's. I see what you mean."

"Sure, Helen will be easier. But, Charlie, this youngster needs someone strict. His complaint was that I was giving him too much work. I was just beginning to get him to do some work too, damn it! She didn't know the details of what had been going on between the boy and me. She never took the time to find out from me. Now where is the education here? Where is the sticking together of this group that we call educators? There's just not enough backing up of teachers by guidance in general."

"They're not for the teacher," added Charlie.

"I don't say that they should be for one group or another. They should be coolly calculating. They should be truthful, and it's very difficult to be truthful, because you make a lot of enemies that way.

Truthfulness would help education and that should be the aim of all of us, including guidance counselors.

"Take their testing. They test the students primarily so that the administration can say to the parents, 'Now look, this is what we have on your child.' I would like to see something done with all the information they get, instead of it just accumulating in the folders. What does the role of the counselor amount to if they just collect material and put it into a disposal basket? There has to be a real use for it, and if there is no use for it, I can't see the good of it.

"And, unfortunately, testing doesn't take into account much of what the *teacher* would like to see done. So, in essence, the tests aren't really meant to help the teacher or the child, but mainly to help the administration."

"But, Paul, you must admit that guidance has been doing a decent job in placing the children."

"I'll admit that. That's their job; testing and scheduling and that's it, at least in the junior high school."

"What about the handling of personal problems?"

"Charlie, there's very little of that being done here and you know it. The little that's done does very little good, because all they do is refer the student to the school psychologist, who isn't allowed to do anything even though he sees the student. All he can do is refer the child to some agency outside of the school."

"Aren't the counselors able to give direct help?"

"Yes, I think any person, including a teacher, is qualified to do this if he is an emotionally mature person. They can handle minor personal problems, but never by patting the kids on the back, as they do. The counselor has to be a real adult. Most of them here are not adults. Charlie, these days I think many of our teacher friends are going into guidance for the same reason many people have gone into psychology—because they're disturbed themselves. Then, of course, there are some others who want it strictly as a steppingstone to administration."

"Guidance represents a semi-administrative post."

"Sure, Charlie, and I can at least accept that type of person. But these disturbed ones. They're the ones that frighten me. Like Claire Trest, now! She's just a child dealing with a child. She's over-protecting this boy, because she quite probably feels very insecure herself. She forgets that she's in a practical situation, not a dream world. Counselors have a tendency to overprotect a child who often doesn't even really want their protection—who is actually groping to understand the world—but when he sees the counselor, the counselor softsoaps him into a need for protection that he doesn't even really want. And many of the teachers are playing right into this ridiculous situation. They send a child to the guidance office because he's acted up in class and encourage these counselors to give the kid a couple of pats on the back and to hold him out of class. This makes the teacher feel good, but it's foolish. This in the name of education? Education, to my mind, should be made of sterner stuff!"

"You mean, some of the teachers have been doing that? Sending kids down for a pat on the back?"

"Yes, Charlie, for a pat on the back. That's what the kids get. They get a pat on the back and are sent to class, supposedly cured of whatever ailed them!"

"Is this common? I haven't heard of it."

"Quite common, I'm sure. More common than most people realize, I think. And when they treat these students like babies, they're doing them a tremendous injustice. It's a travesty to everybody concerned, including the counselors themselves. Charlie, if your kid rode his bike down the middle of the highway and said to all the drivers, 'Watch out for me; I'm on my bike; get out of my way!' and everybody jumped, the kid would soon get the idea that this is the way life is; he gives orders and adults jump! Certainly your kid would not grow up into adulthood knowing how to live with other adults. Yet this kind of action is being encouraged right here in this school.

"But it isn't all guidance's fault. Our dear school administration hasn't stepped in to put a halt to these proceedings. The administration perpetuates this softsoaping approach. The students come to me with notes from guidance to be let out of my class to go to band. I have nothing to say about it. Administration supports that kind of thing."

"So what can be done?" Charlie asked, looking helpless.

"I don't know. If the school would only realize that the teacher sees a student every day, all year, and has all kinds of interaction with that student, and if guidance would only ask the teacher about a case before action was taken, I might not have this bad taste in my mouth."

Role-playing suggestions

[1]

CHARACTERS

PAUL LANDSDALE, *teacher-protagonist*

HELEN CARDEN, *guidance counselor*

SITUATION

Carden and Landsdale are meeting in an empty classroom. Carden is having difficulty in explaining why she changed a student's class (see case). Landsdale, in character, is irked.

[2]

PAUL LANDSDALE

ROSE HOLLY, *teacher*

CAROL SHAW, *teacher*

CLAUDE REESE, *teacher*

At a faculty picnic, Landsdale takes issue with Reese, who feels guidance has "always backed me." Shaw and Holly take sides.

Issue leads

The importance of consulting with the teacher when changing one of his student's program.

How test results can aid the teacher.

Effectively sharing test data.

The qualifications of a classroom teacher to offer personal counseling.

Mr. Roeder's sympathetic ear

. Mrs. Pollack, the home economics teacher, frowned as she inspected Carmella Garcia's handiwork. "Carmella, these stitches are much too far apart. I'm sorry, but they'll have to come out. If you'd only listened to the preliminary instructions that I gave to the class yesterday," she chided.

A sudden rage overcame Carmella; she jumped out of her seat, reached for her books, and with an air of great indignation said, "Mrs. Pollack, you're doing it again. You're doing it again! You're picking on me. I'm going to see Mr. Roeder."

The class was aghast. Mrs. Pollack, maintaining self-control only by great effort, said, "Yes, Carmella, you're going to see your guidance counselor, but you're not marching out of here now! We're both going to see him, but at the end of the period."

Esther Pollack had been teaching home economics for twelve years at Hamilton Junior High. Hamilton was a relatively small school, and she was the "home ec" department. The guidance department was a one-man operation too. Bertram Roeder personified guidance at Hamilton Junior High. "Guidance can't really be as clandestine and mysterious as Roeder makes it out to be," thought Esther Pollack. Hence she had enrolled in a graduate course in guidance, "just to find out more about it."

Roeder portrayed his relationship with the students as one of "great confidentiality." Occasionally he would ask Mrs. Pollack for written reports about the work and attitudes of certain students. He would never share the actual reports of the other teachers. On more than one occasion, he had said to Mrs. Pollack that she was the *only* teacher that was having trouble with a certain student. It was just by coincidence, in talking with some of the student's other teachers, that she found that they too were usually experiencing similar difficulties with the student. Obviously, someone wasn't entirely truthful!

Roeder kept many things to himself. It was difficult and sometimes impossible to gain access to a student's cumulative record. He was a cautious guardian of their records; and in keeping with this kind of approach, whatever students discussed with him was totally sacrosanct. Roeder was the student's great protector. "Maybe that's the role of the counselor," speculated Esther Pollack, "but it certainly seems that he's picking sides. I don't mean to usurp Roeder's position as a specialist, but I thought we were both interested in the same thing—helping the students get a good education! Apparently Roeder wasn't interested in a partnership with the teacher; he was the students' emissary. Wasn't he aware that he often broke into and helped destroy the teacher-student relationship? Roeder would actually come to the teacher and beg on the part of the student: 'I've spoken to the boy, and he's promised me that his attention and work will improve.' What Roeder should have done was to have moved the student to the point where the student came to *me* and asked *me*, 'What can I do to improve?'"

Once Mrs. Pollack tried to discuss her misgivings about Roeder's role with him. He stoically responded, "Mrs. Pollack, in order for me to have the confidence of the child, this is the position my profession calls for me to take."

In the counselor's office the girl was in tears. Mrs. Pollack sat grimly to one side and looked on incredulously as Carmella unfolded her tale of woe and misery to Mr. Roeder's "trained and sympathetic" ear.

"And, Mr. Roeder, the dog ripped the stitching out of the garment and I couldn't finish it any other way . . ."

Mrs. Pollack had heard countless excuses from Carmella throughout the term. She was almost used to them.

"And she—Mrs. Pollack—embarrassed me in front of everyone."

Carmella sobbed and dabbed her liquid eyes with her handkerchief. Mr. Roeder gently walked her to the door and comforted her.

"Don't worry, Carmella. Mrs. Pollack didn't realize the extenuating circumstances involved, and I'm certain that now she does, she's sorry."

Mrs. Pollack looked on in dismay. Roeder was apologizing for her! When he returned, Roeder urged Mrs. Pollack to try to understand Carmella. Mrs. Pollack said that she wouldn't have Carmella back in class until *she* apologized. Mr. Roeder didn't seem to understand. She left at an all too familiar impasse.

Role-playing suggestions

[1]

CHARACTERS	SITUATION
GERTRUDE POLLACK, *teacher-protagonist* BERTRAM ROEDER, *guidance counselor* JOAN WEST, *teacher*	Roeder is meeting with West and Pollack in his office. He explains his theory of the "confidentiality of records." West and Pollack argue that they do not get enough information from Roeder.

[2]

CARMELLA GARCIA, *student* MRS. GARCIA, *Carmella's mother* GERTRUDE POLLACK	Mrs. Garcia and Carmella are meeting with Pollack after school to discuss Carmella's "behavior problems." Mrs. Finn says that in her conference with Mr. Roeder "he didn't think she was such a problem."

Issue leads

The aspects of guidance that would appear "clandestine and mysterious" to a teacher; to a student.

The extent of confidentiality in the counselor-counselee relationship in the public schools.

The degree of accessibility of the cumulative record.

What conditions warrant a guidance counselor to "pick sides."

The advisability of a guidance counselor acting as an emissary of the student.

The pink and rosy world of guidance

"Jimmy Falcon, you old son-of-a-gun! Good to see you! Don't tell me Tuckerton allows even new people to attend conventions!"

"Good to see you again, Mark! Yes, Tuckerton is pretty free with a counselor's time. You see, they don't have to hire a substitute if I'm out! Mark, it's a miracle running into you up here like this."

The two old friends recollected a bit. Then one suggested they leave the crowded lobby of the convention and retire to the adjoining bar to catch up on the recent past.

At a small table near the bar, surrounding two martinis, Jimmy Falcon, a former teacher-counselor at Spencer High and now full-time counselor at prestigious Tuckerton High School, was the first to continue. "Being in guidance is great, Mark. I really enjoy it. When the bell rings, no more hopping to, like Pavlov's dog."

"Jimmy, I only wish I could be such a hypocrite. I'd get into your racket myself!"

"You're kidding."

"I wish I were. Maybe it's different at your new place; but honestly, Jimmy, as you know, the counselors and guidance at Spencer are the world's biggest bunch of hypocrites. They're dishonest; they live in a pink, rosy, unreal world. They're hypocrites. What I can't stand most of all is that they give preferential treatment!"

Jimmy whitened under the attack. He took a big gulp of his martini and asked, "For instance?"

"Well, take Roger Trangel; you remember him. I think he used to be in your salesmanship class when you were at Tuckerton." Jimmy nodded. "Did you know that he spent all of last year in jail or in a reform school for forcing himself on a girl?" Jimmy expressed shock. "This year, Jimmy, he's back with us. Now, while he was in jail the guidance department arranged for him to take his tests, his homework, and everything else. I didn't approve of it at the time; I still don't. I hate the boy. All right. So they go out of the way; they make the teachers send this boy the tests, the homework, and he passes his junior year!"

"While he was in jail?"

"Yes, while he was in jail. He passed his tests and everything else. Okay! The kid studied. He comes back to school and he's kept his nose pretty clean, because if he goes away again he's had it! Now he went into the guidance office to arrange to meet with one of those college representatives this spring, and guidance wouldn't allow him the appointment. 'Sorry, Roger, all interviews are filled.' Now, Jimmy, this was an injustice as far as this kid was concerned. Why give him a chance to make up work when he should be getting zero and then, when it comes down to trying for college, refuse to let him try? They said to him that they were all filled up for appointments to meet with the representatives, but they let other kids in after that! He's the scum of the earth, but he's got as much right as anybody else. They're hypocrites in that guidance office."

"Did he meet the requirements for college?" Jimmy asked.

"I assume he did. But even if he didn't meet the requirements, they should have told him that he didn't instead of saying, 'No, we can't give you an appointment with the representative.'"

"You mean, Mark, they were dishonest?"

"That's the feeling I got, and I think they're a bunch of asses up there."

"Yeah?"

"I'll tell you a person who I think is one of the better guidance counselors there—that's Ed Sus, believe it or not!"

"Ed!" Jimmy said with obvious surprise.

"Yeah. Sure, he's one of the most wishy-washy, spineless individuals that you'll ever meet in a long time, but I've been in conferences where he's talked quite frankly with the kid. 'Look, kid, you've spent three years in this school and you've done nothing. You've jerked around, you've goofed off, and now you tell me you want to go to college! What have you done to earn this right?' I approve of this kind of talk. I think it's fair. 'You want to go to college? All right. I'll send a transcript, but I think you should join the Army.' Or, 'I think you should go out and get a job!' "

"In other words, he's honest."

"Yes; I don't like this talking in those big philosophical terms. I can do it; I don't. I guess I'm crusading against all of civilization this year, but I'm just very upset with the hypocrisy of people."

"But, Mark, how can you generalize from a single incident?"

"You know damned well this kind of thing goes on all the time. We have four different honor rolls at Spencer. Four honor rolls! Listen, if school is to teach kids about life, then these kids have got to learn to fail as well as succeed. Life sometimes means failing. At Spencer, the school and guidance don't let anyone fail. Jimmy, 24 students failed my history course last year. Duffy said, 'Mark, try to cut your failures to about 15.' I thought to myself, if I have to falsify the grades of 10, I might as well go all the way. Jimmy, no one failed my course last year. If Spencer is going to have hypocrites, they might as well be big ones!

"People, counselors, walk away from problems. Tell Vance about a disturbed kid that's wrecking your class. He'll say, 'I didn't know he was disturbed.' But, damn it, it's his job to know! Parents attack teachers in interviews, and guidance lets it go by. They run to the principal with tales.

"Jimmy, you're probably a decent counselor. Don't get me wrong; you're a regular guy. Don't get mixed up with all of that philosophy; be human. Remember, you're not a judge; you're a helper. Jimmy, I've been talking about Spencer, but I think, by and large, the majority of guidance counselors are probably this way. Jimmy, they all read the same books. They all come from the same mold around here. I'm sure that if I sat down and talked with 200 counselors, I'd walk away feeling a 150 of 'em fit what I've just said. The other 50 might be half-way decent."

Jimmy looked down at his empty martini glass. He motioned the waiter for another, this time a *double*.

Role-playing suggestions

[1]

CHARACTERS

MARK VERNON, *teacher-protagonist*
SAL GORCEY, *guidance counselor*
ROGER TRANGEL, *student*

SITUATION

Trangel has asked Vernon help him get into college, because "my counselor isn't trying." Vernon and Gorcey take opposite stands on the advisability of helping Trangel.

[2]

MARK VERNON
ED SUS, *guidance counselor*
JIM GRIFFITHS, *teacher*

Griffiths, in the faculty room, comments to Sus about the "fine work your department is doing." Vernon, sitting by, speaks out in character.

Issue leads

The pressures upon teachers from guidance to pass certain students.

The "unreal" world of counselors.

It's in process

The bell rang. There was a mad scurrying in the halls. Joe Clyne, a business teacher at Oakhurst High, and his close friend and colleague, Art McDougal, walked through the door marked "Faculty."

"Coffee?" Art asked.

"No," Clyne replied. "I'm just too burned up to drink anything."

"Have a little coffee; it's good in slowing you down." Art picked up two plastic-coated paper cups, filled them both with dark coffee, and motioned Joe to a corner of the faculty room. Several other teachers were in the room now, and the mild hum of relaxed "free period" conversation replaced the din of commotion in the hall. Both men sat down.

"Why are you so upset?" Art asked softly.

"That Chisolm boy is still in my business math class, Arty. Nothing is being done."

"Who is his guidance counselor? He's an 11th-grader, isn't he?"

"His counselor is Loretta Burke, but I don't know if it's her fault or the fault of the system. I reported to Loretta way back in October, six months ago, that in my opinion, Barry Chisolm was going to crack up—have a nervous breakdown. I wasn't the first teacher to notice that he was different. That he was going to crack up was only my opinion, but it was based on observation—watching his actions in the classroom. And, from some of his statements, I think he has suicidal tendencies and might do real harm to himself."

"Well, what did guidance do?"

"Oh, he was seen by Mrs. Burke, and she referred him to the school psychologist, but the psychologist, of course, is busy. Something is wrong here! Six months and nothing! What's more, Arty, this isn't the first time that the guidance department has given me the business. The counselors make such very bad mistakes. It makes you wonder if they know what they're doing downstairs. Last year, believe it or not, I had a boy in my bookkeeping class with cerebral palsy. His arm was misshapen; he could hardly write; he had poor coordination. Well, you know the symptoms! And there he was in Bookkeeping I! Obviously the counselor didn't know what the curriculum was in Bookkeeping I—the amount of writing involved on the part of the student and that he has to look at numbers and place them in the correct columns! Actually the boy became very frustrated and was failing the course, and yet, in my heart, I felt that I didn't want this boy to fail. I felt that frustration and failure would be bad for him, so I went down to the guidance department, and finally the boy's parents were called in, and he was removed from my class."

By now Joe Clyne was beginning to unveil a host of feelings. "Some of these counselors don't realize at all what it is like in the classroom. They're way up in the clouds. They've forgotten! You know it's easy to forget. It only takes one year to forget. From what I've seen, most of them are refugees from the classroom. From what they tell me, they wanted to get away from students. They didn't like the classroom, and now they're guiding the very same students they wanted to get away from. It would seem to me that every guidance counselor ought to teach one or two classes. They should be guidance "teachers" in the full sense of the word. They should be teaching at the same time. After all, they're dealing with teachers, and it's very, very easy to forget the problems of teachers.

"I get the feeling guidance has some sort of production quota. The quota is to get a certain number of students into college, and this is their main objective. So they're really a subsidiary of the college admissions offices."

"Yes," Art said, "But why are you so upset this morning?"

"That's just it, Arty. They're not taking first things first. If sending kids to college comes before helping a kid like Barry Chisolm—a kid with a serious emotional problem—certainly their objectives have been distorted completely. Every time I ask about the case, Loretta Burke gets out folders and files and says, 'It's in the process.' In the meantime, Barry Chisolm is still in my class. Oh, he's no discipline problem. I'm not trying to throw him out. He just sits their gazing out of the window or puts his head down and goes to sleep. He takes tests, but he either tears up the test at the end of the period, or he doesn't hand in the paper. This is a serious case. He mumbles unintelligibly and never shows any emotion. Arty, I can't talk to him. Today was the payoff. I walked up to him and offered to give him some help after school. All he could do was shrug his shoulders helplessly. I felt just awful for him.

"Arty, maybe I feel a little disappointed in myself, because my relationship with most students is very, very good. Usually I can kid with a student. I don't have any real discipline problems. Usually I can kid a student and get some sort of smile or reaction. With him, it's completely frustrating. Maybe it's my frustration I'm transferring to him! I'm starting to sound like an amateur psychologist.

"You know, I've heard her jump out of her seat when she opened the mail and saw Susie Y was admitted to Radcliffe. 'I got one into Radcliffe!' Maybe it's the pressures of our society today. These people just don't seem to have enough time for the real problems. I know that the guidance counselor is in the middle. He gets the pressure from the parents. He gets the pressure from the principal. He gets the pressure from the board of education. He gets the pressure from the teacher. But he still has plenty of time to drink coffee, so the pressures and problems can't be as great as they seem to be." Joe's neck was red with anger.

"I very seldom blow my top, Arty, but I'm going down to Mrs. Burke and tell her exactly what I think, and maybe I'll finally get some help for this poor boy."

Joe got up, prepared to head directly to Mrs. Burke's office. "She's already told me to my face that I don't like guidance. Boy, is she right!"

Role-playing suggestions

[1]

CHARACTERS

JOE CLYNE, *teacher-protagonist*
LORETTA BURKE, *guidance counselor*

SITUATION

Clyne, after the scene portrayed in the case, has left the faculty room. He finds Burke in her office and begins to rail against her and guidance. She defends her position.

[2]

JOE CLYNE
LORETTA BURKE
FRANK LORENZO, *school
　psychologist*
AL CORRIGAN, *principal*

Corrigan, hearing of the
referral problem, has invited
Clyne, Burke, and Lorenzo to his
office in order "to get to the
bottom" of the problem. Clyne
describes the situation
in character.

Issue leads

The importance of the teacher's referral
role.

The advisability of guidance counselors teaching one or two
classes regularly.

case **25**

They've got all the numbers, but they don't know the score
Look, I've been in the education field over 25 years. I've been a classroom teacher most of that time, but I've also been a department head, assistant principal, advisor to seniors, and so forth. So far as I have been able to determine, the heart of education is in the classroom, between student and teacher. Teachers are it. All those other jobs—curriculum advisors, coordinators, and yes, guidance counselors—they're basically parasitic. They exist off the teachers' sweat.

Take guidance. Now your best guidance counselor is the classroom teacher. As a teacher, I've been a father confessor, a parent substitute. It's amazing when a youngster has confidence in you—the problems he'll bring to you. With all my experience with kids, all these years, I can spot a troubled youngster without too much difficulty. You can sense certain symptoms and patterns of behavior.

Now these guidance people will lead you to believe that they are helping kids with personal problems. Frankly, they aren't close enough to the kids to really help. They see a youngster every once in a while, but for how long? Ten or twenty minutes? The classroom teacher sees that same youngster day in and day out all year. We overhear comments about his family; we see how he gets along on committees; we see his dress habits, his school work, everything. And you're going to tell me that the guidance counselor can help the kids more than we can! Bosh.

All the counselor knows about the student as an individual is

102

from test scores. You can't talk reason at all to a guidance counselor if he's got test scores in front of him. He's got all the cold figures, graphs, and tables on students, but he doesn't deal enough with the warm bodies. Naturally, it's often more comfortable and secure for the guidance counselor to hide behind all his charts and graphs. Illustration: I went to a guidance person about a student in my physics class who had clearly demonstrated day in and day out that he couldn't do the work. The guidance person pulled out his quantitative analysis of the student and said, 'Yes, but his tests show he has the potential!' That was the extent of his service. Now honestly!

Physics requires a thorough background in math. Guidance has allowed many of the wrong students in there. The blasted counselor thinks physics is the same course he took 20 years ago when he was in high school. But it's changed, and he should make it his business to find out the changes if he's going to recommend kids for the course. Especially the head of guidance. He's got a Ph.D. or an Ed.D.! He should know the changes.

Frankly, I just haven't, in my 25 years in education, met any member of the whole psychiatric team that could do as good a job of reaching students as a good classroom teacher. As far as my contacts with guidance are concerned, I have as little contact as possible. Guidance is not a resource for me.

Role-playing suggestions

[1]

CHARACTERS

LLOYD CLARKE, *teacher-protagonist*
EVERETT BREWER, *guidance counselor*

SITUATION

Clarke encounters Brewer in the school corridor. Brewer requests information about a student who has been placed in Clarke's physics class. Clarke states that the student has been "sadly misplaced." A heated discussion ensues between Clarke and Brewer.

[2]

LLOYD CLARKE
EVERETT BREWER
MRS. ESTHER LEVITT, *parent*

Clarke, Brewer, and Mrs. Levitt are in a joint conference, regarding her son Charles. Mrs. Levitt feels that Clarke "doesn't really understand" her son, who is in Clarke's science class. Brewer, trying to help, explains "some unusual background factors in Charles' record" to Clarke. Clarke reacts in character.

Issue leads

The "parasitic" nature of non-teaching personnel.

Who does the "real" guidance—teacher, counselor, or both?

A comparison of a teacher's and a counselor's contacts with students.

The extent that guidance counselors "hide" behind test data.

Bibliography

ATWOOD, MARK, "An Anthropological Approach to Administrative Change: The Introduction of a Guidance Program in a High School." Unpublished doctoral dissertation, Teachers College, Columbia University, 1960.

BALINSKY, BENJAMIN, and ANGELO DISPENZIERI, "An Evaluation of the Lecture and the Role Playing Methods in the Development of Interviewing Skills," *Personnel and Guidance Journal,* 39 (March, 1961), 583-85.

BERGMANN, RICHARD B., and WILLIAM M. WRIGHT, "A Guide to Role-Playing." Doctor of Education Project Report, Teachers College, Columbia University, 1955.

BUCHER, RUE, CHARLES E. FRITZ, and E. L. QUARANTELLI, "Tape Recorded Interviews in Social Research," *American Sociological Review,* 21 (June, 1956), 359-64.

BYRNE, RICHARD H., "Situational Cases for Training School Counselors." Doctor of Education Project Report, Teachers College, Columbia University, 1952.

COPELAND, MELVIN T., "The Genesis of the Case Method," in *The Case Method at the Harvard Business School,* ed. Malcolm P. McNair. New York: McGraw-Hill Book Company, 1954.

COX, ROBERT L., "Where is Our First Obligation?" *The School Counselor,* 12 (March, 1965), 159-60.

DARLEY, JOHN G., "The Faculty is Human, Too," *Personnel and Guidance Journal,* 35 (December, 1956), 225-30.

ESCOTT, STANLEY B., "The Counselor-Teacher Relationship," *The School Counselor,* 11 (May, 1964), 215-20.

FAUST, IRVIN, "As They See It: A Casebook of Student-Centered Studies as Projected Through the Author." Doctor of Education Project Report, Teachers College, Columbia University, 1960.

FRENCH, JOHN R. P., "Retraining an Autocratic Leader," *Journal of Abnormal and Social Psychology*, 39 (April, 1944), 224-37.

GETZELS, JACOB W., and HERBERT A. THELAN, "The Classroom as a Unique Social System," National Society for the Study of Education, Fifty-Ninth Yearbook, Part II. Chicago: The Society, 1960.

GORDON, IRA J., *The Teacher as a Guidance Worker*. New York: Harper and Row, Publishers, 1956. 350 pp.

HUDD, ROGER T., "The Dean is a Marginal Man," *The Journal of Educational Sociology*, 35 (December, 1961), 145-51.

JOHNSTON, EDGAR G., MILDRED PETERS, and WILLIAM EVRAIFF, *The Role of the Teacher in Guidance*. Englewood Cliffs, N. J.: Prentice-Hall, Inc., 1959. 276 pp.

KLEIN, ALAN F., *Role Playing in Leadership Training and Group Problem Solving*. New York: Association Press, 1956. 176 pp.

KNAPP, DALE L., and EARL W. DENNY, "The Counselor's Responsibility in Role Definition," *Personnel and Guidance Journal*, 40 (September, 1961), 48-50.

LIPPITT, ROSEMARY, and ANNE HUBBELL, "Role Playing for Personnel and Guidance Workers: Review of the Literature with Suggestions for Applications," *Group Psychotherapy*, 9 (August, 1956), 89-114.

LLOYD-JONES, ESTHER, RUTH BARRY, and BEVERLY WOLF, eds., *Case Studies in College Student-Staff Relationships*. New York: Teachers College, Columbia University, 1956. 117 pp.

LLOYD-JONES, ESTHER, and ESTHER WESTERVELT, eds., *Behavioral Science and Guidance: Proposals and Perceptions*. New York: Teachers College, Columbia University, 1963. 128 pp.

MC NAIR, MALCOLM P., ed., *The Case Method at the Harvard Business School*. New York: McGraw-Hill Book Company, 1954. 292 pp.

MORENO, JACOB L.,"Role," in *The Sociometry Reader*, ed. Jacob L. Moreno. New York: The Free Press of Glencoe, Inc., 1960.

PATOUILLET, RAYMOND A., "Working with People in the Development of High School Personnel Work." Doctor of Education Project Report, Teachers College, Columbia University, 1951.

RIBBECK, JAMES C., "Don't Forget the Classroom Teacher," *The School Counselor*, 12 (December, 1964), 98-100.

ROEBER, EDWARD C., GLENN E. SMITH, and CLIFFORD E. ERICKSON, *Or-*

ganization and Administration of Guidance Services. New York: Thomas Y. Crowell Company, 1955. 294 pp.

RODEHAVER, MYLES W., WILLIAM B. AXTELL, and RICHARD E. GROSS, *The Sociology of the School.* New York: Thomas Y. Crowell Company, 1957. 262 pp.

RUSSELL, JAMES G., and ARTHUR R. WILLIS, "Survey of Teachers' Opinions of Guidance Services," *Personnel and Guidance Journal,* 42 (March, 1964), 707-9.

STEWART, JAMES A., "Factors Influencing Teacher Attitudes Toward and Participation in Guidance Services," *Personnel and Guidance Journal,* 39 (May, 1961), 729-34.

SHERIF, MUZAFER, ed., *Intergroup Relations and Leadership.* New York: John Wiley & Sons, Inc., 1962. 284 pp.

STRONG, RUTH, *The Role of the Teacher in Personnel Work.* New York: Teachers College, Columbia University, 1953. 491 pp.

WHITE, ERWIN W., "An Analysis of the Attitudes of Counselors in North Carolina Schools Concerning Their Required Training." Unpublished doctoral dissertation, University of North Carolina, 1962.

WILLEY, ROY D., and MELVIN DUNN, *The Role of the Teacher in the Guidance Program.* Bloomington, Ill.: McKnight and McKnight, 1964. 487 pp.

Appendix

The reader should find Table 1 helpful in determining, at a glance, those cases that deal with areas appropriate to his particular objectives. The table lists the areas that concerned the case protagonists during the original interviews, together with case numbers in which the concern is reflected. It should be understood that although each area of concern has been represented by a negative statement in the table, the concern was not necessarily reflected negatively in each case. For example, the first area of concern, "He's forgotten what it was like in the classroom," is represented in positive, rather than negative form in case 2. Case 2 reflects a counselor who *remembers* what it was like in the classroom.

TABLE I

Statements Representing Areas of Concern to Selected Classroom Teachers Interviewed Regarding Their Attitudes Toward Guidance and Guidance Counselors

STATEMENTS REPRESENTING AREAS OF CONCERN	CASE NUMBERS
Counselors' Attitudes Toward Classroom Teachers	
He has forgotten what it was like in the classroom.	1, 2, 7, 9, 11, 12, 13, 15, 16, 18, 19, 20, 21, 24
He does not reciprocate the help that I give.	1, 2, 5, 6, 7, 8, 11, 12, 13, 18, 19, 20, 21, 22
He does not realize that he does not fully understand the nature of my subject.	2, 3, 7, 9, 11, 12, 13, 15, 17, 18, 20, 21, 23, 24

109

He is not on my side.

1, 2, 7, 9, 11, 16, 17, 18, 19, 20, 21, 22, 23

He thinks that I am not able to comprehend his tests, etc.

1, 2, 4, 6, 10, 13, 15, 18, 19, 20, 21, 22, 23

He is often tactless, hence he places teachers in awkward positions.

1, 2, 6, 12, 14, 15, 18, 20, 21, 22, 23

He often lets me down because he's afraid of parents.

1, 2, 7, 9, 11, 16, 17, 19, 21, 23

He wants to weaken my course, without being realistic about the objectives and purposes of my course.

1, 3, 9, 11, 12, 16, 17, 21, 22, 24

He doesn't let me know what he has done when I refer someone.

2, 6, 13, 17, 18, 19, 20, 22, 24

He does not understand and respect the pressures of time that I feel during the school day.

1, 2, 8, 16, 17, 18, 19, 21

He has been unprofessional in letting lay persons denigrate me, without coming to my defense.

1, 7, 17, 19, 21, 22, 23

I have to wait too long before my referrals are seen by him.

6, 15, 21, 24

Counselors' Attitudes Toward Students

He over-protects students.

1, 2, 7, 8, 9, 11, 15, 16, 17, 18, 19, 21, 22, 23, 24

He lacks warmth which often makes him insensitive to the student's real needs.

1, 4, 5, 6, 8, 11, 12, 14, 17, 20, 21, 24

He gives insufficient attention to those in need of personal counseling.

1, 2, 4, 5, 6, 13, 16, 20, 21, 24

He doesn't really know the students very well.

1, 2, 5, 13, 15, 18, 19, 20, 21

He is too highly oriented toward college admissions counseling.

3, 5, 6, 16, 20, 21, 24

He is apathetic when it comes to taking a stand in behalf of a particular youngster if it "rocks the boat."

1, 5, 6, 14, 20, 23

He rarely attracts kids voluntarily to his office.

1, 5, 13, 20, 23

He gives preferential treatment to certain types of students.

1, 4, 21, 23, 24

He usually acts as a judge, rather than a helper of students. — 1, 4, 6, 21, 23

He makes college recommendations without carefully considering the suitability of the college for a particular student. — 1, 5, 23

He fosters unnecessary competition among the students. — 12

Professional Competency and Effectiveness of Guidance Counselors

He typifies all the weaknesses in the American system of education. — 1, 9, 14, 15, 16, 17, 18, 19, 20, 21, 22, 23, 24

I—not the counselor—do the real guidance. — 1, 2, 5, 9, 13, 15, 18, 19, 20, 21

He is overly confidential regarding his work. — 1, 6, 12, 15, 18, 19, 20, 21, 22

He occasionally provides an adequate diagnosis of a student's problems, but rarely, if ever, any remedies. — 1, 5, 9, 15, 17, 18, 19, 21

A competent clerk can do much that this "high priced" counselor does. — 1, 5, 6, 9, 11, 15, 20, 21

He has too much free time. — 1, 6, 13, 14, 17, 18, 21, 24

He does not have the training or knowledge that would qualify him to help anyone with his emotional problems. — 1, 9, 11, 15, 17, 19, 20

Practically all he does is scheduling. — 1, 2, 5, 6, 11, 20, 21

He makes extremely serious mistakes when he makes them. — 7, 14, 15, 19, 21, 23, 24

He adequately performs college placement tasks, but little else. — 1, 5, 9, 11, 20, 24

Even though he is qualified, he does not do any personal-social counseling. — 1, 5, 20, 21, 24

I have no professional contact with him. — 1, 17, 18, 20

Counselors' Private Attitudes Toward Self and Job

He probably feels inferior—tries too hard to make himself important. — 1, 4, 10, 12, 13, 15, 16, 20, 22

He is deceitful with himself, as well as with others.	1, 5, 7, 8, 9, 14, 21, 22, 23
He has a pseudo-psychological jargon all his own.	1, 8, 14, 15, 19, 22, 23
He's in guidance because he couldn't teach.	2, 5, 8, 14, 24
He is an insincere person.	1, 5, 8, 12, 23
He is in guidance only as a step to administration, and not because he is truly dedicated to guidance work.	1, 20, 21, 24, 25
He is in guidance work primarily for extra money, rather than because of his interest or dedication.	1, 6, 13, 14, 20
He is in the field primarily because he has many "problems" of his own; he is an emotionally immature person.	1, 15, 21, 23